Rails Along the Derwent

The Story of the Derwent Valley Light Railway

Jonathan D. Stockwell
and
Ian Drummond

Foreword by
Paul Atterbury

Holne Publishing

© Holne Publishing, Jonathan D. Stockwell & Ian Drummond 2013
British Library Cataloguing in Publication Data
A record for this book is available from the British Library
ISBN 978-0-9563317-6-2
Published by: Holne Publishing, PO Box 343, LEEDS, LS19 9FW
Typesetting and Photo Restoration by: Holne Publishing Services, PO Box 343, LEEDS, LS19 9FW
Printed by: Charlesworth Press, Flanshaw Way, Flanshaw Lane, Wakefield, WF2 9LP

Reasonable efforts have been made to discover the true copyright owners of the photographs reproduced in this volume, and no infringement of copyright is intended. If you have any evidence about the copyright owner of any photograph, or the photographer of any photograph listed as 'photographer unknown', please contact the publisher in the first instance.

Photographs in this volume have been digitally adjusted to enhance clarity, and also remove blemishes, dust etc. However, no intentional alterations have been made to affect their historical significance.

Except where indicated plans and drawings are from the Derwent Valley Light Railway Society Archive housed at the Yorkshire Museum of Farming, Murton Park, York. Approximate scales are given where known, and unless indicated otherwise the top edge of maps and plans is north.

The southern terminus of the Derwent Valley Light Railway is at various points referred to as either Cliff Common or Cliffe Common, for the purposes of this volume we have standardised on Cliff Common.

Holne Publishing
PO Box 343
LEEDS
LS19 9FW
enquiries@holnepublishing.co.uk
www.holnepublishing.co.uk

Cover Photos:

Front: On 27 September 1963 ex-LMS Ivatt 2-6-0 No.46409 approaches Osbaldwick Road crossing with a joint Railway Correspondence and Travel Society (RCTS) and Stephenson Locomotive Society (SLS) special. The overgrown nature of the track was typical of the railway at the time, and the crossing keeper is growing some fine vegetables on the lineside. In the left rear background can be glimpsed the cement plant at Osbaldwick station.

Back: Class 03 BR diesel shunter D2112, on hire to the Derwent Valley Light Railway (DVLR), passes the line's solitary signal on the approach to Wheldrake station with the daily pick up goods on 21 July 1964. This signal must have been the most photographed in Britain as it was 'snapped' by countless visitors to the line. The train includes the line's again much-photographed ex-South Eastern and Chatham Railway (SECR) birdcage brake van.

(Both Photos: David J. Mitchell)

Contents

Above: On 27 September 1963 ex-LMS Ivatt 2-6-0 No.46409 pulls onto the Derwent Valley Light Railway at York (Layerthorpe) station at the head of the joint RCTS/SLS railtour. This was on a five day tour of the North East, which had just started from York station. The train travelled down to Cliff Common, and it will be seen at various locations as it made its way down the line.

(Photo: David J. Mitchell)

Foreword

Above: A typical working portrait of the Derwent Valley Light Railway as BR class J25 No.65714 stands at York (Layerthorpe) station c. 1957.

(Photo: David A. Lawrence Copyright Colour-Rail 309060)

At its peak, Britain's railway map included a surprising number of minor independent lines, usually brought to life by a mixture of local ambition, enthusiasm and optimism, much of which remained largely unfulfilled. Yet, quite a number enjoyed long lives, with some escaping both the 1923 Grouping and the formation of British Railways. In the course of years of researching and writing about railways, I have come across a number of these railways, and I have always enjoyed exploring their history, visiting the remains of their routes and including them in my books.

The Derwent Valley Light Railway is a classic example, owing its existence, like so many, to the famous Light Railway Act of 1896. This Act, encouraging as it did the building of low-cost, simply operated railways catering for largely local needs, brought lines into many quiet corners of Britain, and significantly expanded the nation's railway network between 1900 and the 1920s.

Many of these railways subsequently faded away after a few decades of quiet and unremarkable life, leaving just memories and some traces on the landscape. The DVLR was not one of these and continued to operate, albeit in a fragmented and frequently financially challenged form, until the 1980s, serving a variety of constantly changing local needs. Unlike many of the less successful lines, the DVLR realised quite early in its life that passenger carrying was uneconomic and so concentrated on freight traffic from the 1920s. This was the key to its survival over a long period, though it was greatly helped by the comings and goings of many industries and other commercial activities established along the route, which included agriculture, coal, oil and petroleum, chemicals, concrete, storage and the needs of the military. As such, the railway was able to enjoy a long life and make a significant contribution to local history.

In common with some other former Light Railways, the DVLR has been brought back to life by enthusiasts and now operates as a heritage railway. Track has been relaid, rolling stock acquired and restored, and a station building saved and rebuilt. The result gives modern visitors much pleasure and a sense of how it must have been when this railway was in its heyday.

This book, which has been produced as part of the celebrations that mark the Derwent Valley Light Railway's centenary in 2013, brings the story of the railway to life. I am very pleased to write this foreword, and thus to be a small part of the process that ensures that the story of this important and fiercely independent local railway is not forgotten.

Paul Atterbury

Introduction

Above: Encounter at a crossing: The last regular working to Wheldrake meets one of the local farmers at an occupation crossing south of Elvington on 14 May 1968. This photograph featured in the booklet, mentioned below, purchased by one of the authors during his first visit to the line in 1979. (Photo: R. Wildsmith)

The Derwent Valley Light Railway (DVLR) has always fascinated me, and happily I did travel on its remains. In fact it was on the final day of normal timetabled steam passenger trains on 31 August 1979. Little did I know some thirty-plus years later I would be involved in writing its updated history in the centenary year.

Without doubt the DVLR has had a remarkable history. As the last Company chairman, Roy Cook, wrote in a booklet, which was purchased on the aforementioned visit: "with its one signal, the DVLR was unique in having survived two world wars, the railway groupings, nationalisation, post war depressions and crises. Yet it was able to pay a dividend continuously from 1941". It also provided a healthy return for its shareholders when the Company sold its assets in the mid 1980's.

Despite the original passenger services ceasing in 1926 three stations still survive today. Even more incredulous are the number of tickets still in existence. A few years ago I purchased various tickets on 'eBay', and by chance a number of interesting examples came up for sale, some were won and some lost (a number of the former gracing these pages). However, further investigations revealed that the seller's father had been the railway's general manager, the tickets having been 'play things' for both her and her children! Needless to say contact was made and artefacts as well as memories were shared with the Society.

I must thank all those who have kindly made their photographs, artefacts and memories available to the DVLR Society. Without their help this book would not have been possible. I am particularly indebted to the former Company directors, employees and their families, who freely gave their time in interviews. This included unlimited access to various family photo albums. They have also donated various items of DVLR memorabilia. In fact 'a treasure trove of material' came to light only a couple of months ago, just in time for this book.

For those who "saw the DVLR" I trust this book will bring back memories, and to those who did not, that it gives an insight as to what a unique railway it was. I also hope that you will visit the DVLR Society at Murton Park, where the spirit and determination of the DVLR lives on. Part of the profits of this book will be going towards the work there.

Thanks also go to my co-author and publisher, Ian, whose faith and patience is endless! Lastly special thanks go to my wife Lesley. She rekindled my interest in the DVLR as we were married at Skipwith Church, and her continuing support has enabled me to carry out this project.

Sadly the original Company minute books appear to have been lost in a fire, with only a few fragments coming to light. Therefore, while we hope this is a comprehensive history, it is not definitive, as there are still gaps in our knowledge. However, I would welcome contact from anyone with further information to be added to the Society's archive.

Jonathan D. Stockwell
(Derwent Valley Light Railway Society Archivist)
June 2013

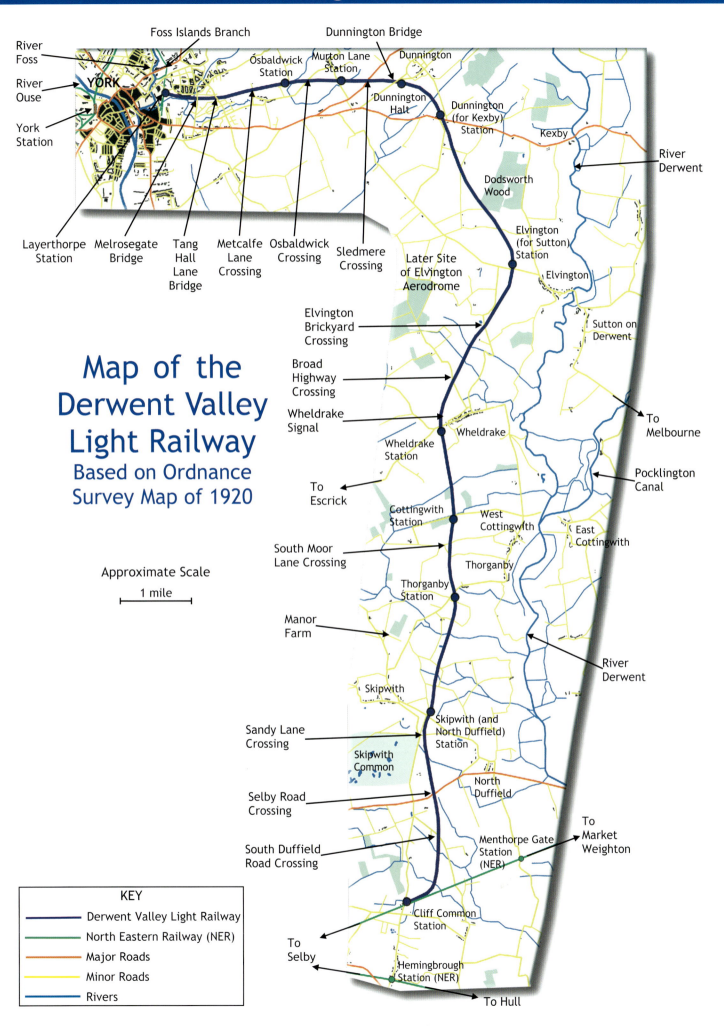

River Foss

Foss Islands Branch

Dunnington Bridge

River Ouse

YORK

Osbaldwick Station

Murton Lane Station

Dunnington

York Station

Dunnington Halt

Dunnington (for Kexby) Station

Kexby

River Derwent

Dodsworth Wood

Layerthorpe Station

Melrosegate Bridge

Tang Hall Lane Bridge

Metcalfe Lane Crossing

Osbaldwick Crossing

Sledmere Crossing

Later Site of Elvington Aerodrome

Elvington (for Sutton) Station

Elvington

Sutton on Derwent

Map of the Derwent Valley Light Railway
Based on Ordnance Survey Map of 1920

Elvington Brickyard Crossing

Broad Highway Crossing

Wheldrake Signal

Wheldrake Station

Wheldrake

To Melbourne

Pocklington Canal

To Escrick

Cottingwith Station

West Cottingwith

East Cottingwith

Approximate Scale

1 mile

South Moor Lane Crossing

Thorganby

Thorganby Station

Manor Farm

River Derwent

Skipwith

Sandy Lane Crossing

Skipwith (and North Duffield) Station

Skipwith Common

Selby Road Crossing

North Duffield

To Market Weighton

South Duffield Road Crossing

Menthorpe Gate Station (NER)

KEY
— Derwent Valley Light Railway
— North Eastern Railway (NER)
— Major Roads
— Minor Roads
— Rivers

Cliff Common Station

To Selby

Hemingbrough Station (NER)

To Hull

Gradient Map of DVLR

(Based on DVLR Gradient Map
Gradients in form of 1 in x)

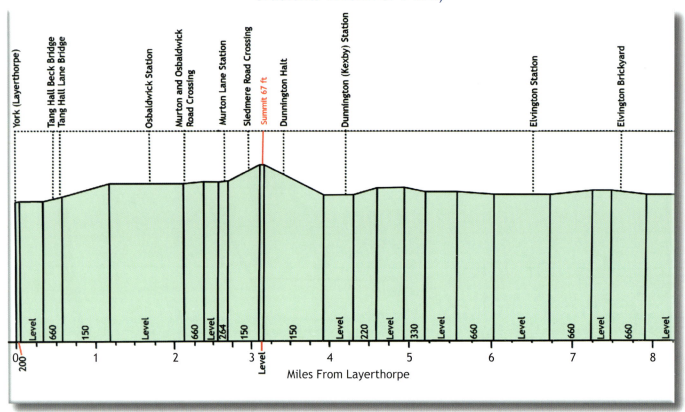

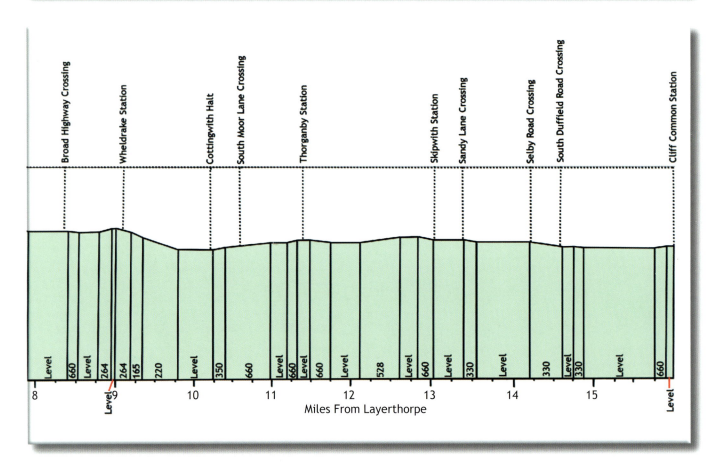

The History of the Derwent Valley Light Railway

Origins and Construction

Introduction

The story of the Derwent Valley Light Railway (DVLR) is one of a railway that was a survivor. It became the last British standard gauge independent Light Railway to operate continuously from pre-grouping days through to the 1980s. In many ways it should not have survived, but it did thanks, in the main, to the entrepreneurial spirit which led to the line's construction, and also to its innovative approach to developing new sources of traffic.

For much of its life it also had a keen sense of being part of the local community, particularly the local farmers, whom it provided with the means of getting their produce to market, even in tough economic times. Of course its independent nature also led to some interesting practices that would not be found on most of the main line railways. This included leaving wagons on the main line between stations for farmers to load, or unload, as necessary. Its lack of main line standard maintenance also probably saved it from a premature end during World War Two.

This then is the story of a resourceful company that could be independent in every sense of the word, and yet which served the area for nearly seventy years. A railway that demands to be wider known.

The Derwent Valley

Meandering from its source on the North York Moors, the River Derwent flows south through Malton continuing on to Stamford Bridge. Then its course takes it south east of York, before meeting the River Ouse near Hemingbrough. East of York it formed the eastern boundary of the Wapentake of Ouse and Derwent.

On the western side of the river valley the land was relatively flat and open. Down it there are scattered villages and hamlets, such as Wheldrake, Cottingwith, Thorganby and Skipwith. Most of these were originally settled by the Angles, with the exception of Thorganby,

which, as its name implies, was settled by Scandinavians, and each has only several hundred inhabitants. Up until the end of the 19th Century, and into the 20th, the main occupation in the area was arable farming.

Changing Transportation Links

Few significant roads crossed the area, but in the early 18th Century the Derwent was made navigable from the Ouse as far as Malton. This meant that barges could transport grain out from the farms, and coal, as well as other commodities, could be brought in. Thus the valley was linked with the wider world through the ports at Goole and Hull.

George Hudson's York and North Midland Railway (Y&NMR) built the first railways in the area. The Company opening a line on 20 May 1839 from York south to the Leeds and Selby line at Gascoigne Wood. Then in July 1845 the Y&NMR opened the first line to cross the Derwent valley, which ran from York to Scarborough via Malton.

This was followed by a line which was proposed to run from York to Beverley, crossing the Derwent at Stamford Bridge. At Beverley the line would link with the Y&NMR's line between Hull and Bridlington. On 4 October 1847 the first section of this line, from York to Market Weighton, was opened. The extension to Beverley having to be postponed due to financing problems. These were to eventually lead to the collapse of George Hudson's 'Empire'. The last of the Y&MNR's lines through the area was the line from Selby to Market Weighton, which opened on 1 August 1848.

After the financial crisis of the Hudson 'Empire' the Y&MNR became part of the North Eastern Railway (NER) in 1854. In turn the NER took over the Derwent Navigation in 1855 and raised the navigation rates. This had the effect of moving goods from water to rail, through the railheads at Malton and Stamford Bridge. Finally, the line between Market Weighton and Beverley opened on 1 May 1865, so trains could run directly between York and Hull.

All this left the Derwent valley east of York, at the centre of a near triangle of NER lines. However, in 1880 another significant line in the history of the DVLR was opened. This was the branch that ran from the York to Scarborough line through the eastern outskirts of York to the area known as Foss Islands. This also served the Rowntree's chocolate factory and York gas works, as well as the cattle market. Originally the line was built for goods, but a passenger service, for employees of the chocolate factory, was operated to Rowntree Halt from 1927 until 1988.

Apparently there was only one previous proposal for a railway along the Derwent valley, although in this case along the eastern bank of the river. *The York Herald* for 17 February 1883 reported on a meeting of the Derwent District Agricultural Club where a Mr Wright, president of the club, spoke in support of the proposed scheme. This was for a line from Howden, where it could connect with the Hull and Barnsley Railway, as well as the NER line between Selby and Hull. From here it would run up the eastern side of the Derwent valley to Stamford Bridge, to connect with the NER York to Market Weighton and

Beverley line. It would then proceed north to Crambe Gate House where it would meet with the York to Scarborough line. But nothing further was heard of this scheme, and the next known development came with the moves to build what would become the DVLR.

Origins of the DVLR

One of the paradoxes of the DVLR is that for a railway that was to become Britain's last independent commercial standard gauge railway, it owed its existence to the public sector, being the only Light Railway that was originally promoted by two local councils. This happened at the end of the 19th Century when a new piece of legislation made the promotion of railways by public bodies possible. The new Act also opened up possibilities for railways to be built where previously they would have been regarded as uneconomic.

This was the Light Railway Act of 1896, and it enabled minor railways to be built under Light Railway Orders (LROs), without the expense of an Act of Parliament. Lines built under a LRO did not have to be standard gauge, but could have sharper curves and steeper gradients. Therefore, there were less earthworks to be constructed and those that were built were on a lesser scale. It also meant that stations could be provided to minimal standards, and level crossings used in place of over or underbridges. However, there was also a maximum speed limit imposed of 25mph.

The Light Railway Act helped with the promotion of a new series of lines. These included the narrow gauge Leek and Manifold Light Railway, and the Welshpool and Llanfair Light Railway, as well as the standard gauge Fawley branch of the Southern Railway. One of the well known proponents of Light Railways was Colonel Stephens, who was involved with a number of lines across the country.

By the 1890s the Derwent valley was a rich farming area, but the farmers needed a cheap, reliable form of transport, not only to transport their produce and livestock to market, but also to bring in the supplies that they needed. The Rural District Council (RDC) of Riccall, which covered part of the Derwent valley, recognised that the lack of transport infrastructure in the area was a limiter on economic growth and development. This put their farmers in particular at a disadvantage compared with those from other areas.

This concern led the Council, on 21 March 1898, to resolve to discuss at their next meeting; 'the question of constructing ... a light railway.... from Barlby railway siding or

Map showing the DVLR and the local NER network

Cliff Common, to Skipwith, North Duffield, Thorganby, West Cottingwith, Wheldrake, Sutton, Newton, Kexby, Dunnington and ending at Stamford Bridge.' They recognised that this would need the support of other councils, and so they decided to contact Escrick RDC to see if they would be interested in participating in such a venture.

Over the coming months discussions were held with various bodies. A deputation was sent to the NER in January 1899 to solicit their support for the scheme. By this point the plan had changed from the line running to Stamford Bridge, to instead joining with the NER at Foss Islands on the outskirts of York.

Local consultations were undertaken, *The Yorkshire Herald* reporting on a meeting held in the schoolroom at Elvington on 17 February 1899. This was to decide on the course of the railway between Dunnington and Wheldrake, the route between the former and York and the latter and Cliff Common having been 'practically settled'. Here it was stated that the NER supported the proposed line, and were willing to facilitate junctions at both Cliff Common and Foss Islands. By a large majority the meeting voted for a route that would bring the proposed line as close to Elvington as possible, in order to serve the villages and farms in that area.

Now the scheme had become a joint project between Riccall and Escrick RDCs. At a special meeting held in May 1899 it was resolved to apply for a Light Railway Order for the construction of the Derwent Valley Light Railway (DVLR). In fact they applied for two lines, the first, known as Railway No.1, was the main line from a junction with the Foss Islands branch on the south side of the Hallfield Road overbridge, to Cliff Common station and was to be 15 miles 7 furlongs and 5 chains in length. Meanwhile the second line, Railway No.2, was a short spur of only 1 furlong 9 chains that would have formed a triangle with the Foss Islands branch.

A public inquiry was held on 29 September 1899 at the York Union board room, led by The Earl of Jersey and Colonel Boughey, both Light Railway Commissioners. At the inquiry, as recorded in *The Yorkshire Herald*, it was stated that the proposed line would serve an area of something like 30,000 acres. Railway No.1 would cost an estimated £69,338 to construct, the bulk of which would be for permanent way materials, while Railway No.2 would cost £2,652, making a total of £71,990.

Another estimate was that the line would carry an annual tonnage of 100,000 of goods. Income was also estimated at £10,000 annually for goods, £250 for cattle and horse-boxes, with £1,250 from

passenger services, making a total of £11,500 per year. Operating costs would account for £6,325, leaving £5,175 in net receipts.

One of the key witnesses for the promoters was local landowner Beilby Lawley, Third Baron Wenlock of Escrick, and also a director of the NER, who would play a key role in the life of the DVLR. He stated that the poor transportation was a hindrance to the local farmers. In particular he highlighted the need for manure to be transported cheaply to the farms, as well as for the potato crop to be transported to market, and that 'the more manure they put into the land the more potatoes they took out'. Lord Wenlock also commented on the state of the local roads making the observation that 'he had very often had to find serious fault with the authorities for the manner in which the roads were kept'. This remark was apparently greeted with laughter from the assembled company. He also hoped that the railway would lead to the development of some of the brickyards in the area.

Objections were also heard, chief of which came from York Corporation and the Ecclesiastical Commissioners who requested the construction of an overbridge at Tang Hall Lane instead of the proposed level crossing. Representations were also made on behalf of Messrs. Hill, Carriers and Tanners, about the effect the proposed line would have on their premises. They stated that the 'advantage of the landowners and ratepayers in Escrick and Riccal ought not to be consulted at the cost of serious expenditure and damage to a citizen of York'.

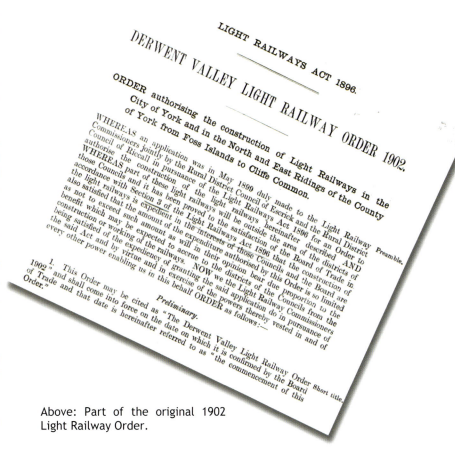

Above: Part of the original 1902 Light Railway Order.

At the end of what was only a four and half hour session, Lord Jersey stated that the Commissioners would recommend the granting of the Order, but that the objections of York Corporation and the Ecclesiastical Commissioners as well as Messrs. Hill should be dealt with. Eventually the order was granted in 1902, and it remained the only case in the country where such powers were granted to local councils. However, it was to be another eleven years before the line was opened.

Delays and Frustration

As intimated the granting of the LRO did not lead to an immediate start on construction. There then followed a frustrating period of arguments, not helped by the death in February 1900 of one of the prominent public supporters of the DVLR George Tindale JP. He had chaired the meeting at Elvington the previous year. Another major stumbling block was the financial obligation that the LRO would have placed on the two councils, Escrick would have been responsible for £60,000 and Riccall £40,000.

Under the terms of the LRO a Joint Committee was established to oversee the construction and operation of

Above: The prospectus for the Derwent Valley Light Railway Company issued in 1910.

the line. This was made up of six members nominated by Escrick council and three by Riccall. However, it soon became clear that the councils would not be able to raise the level of capital required.

However, in 1902 they had established a consultative committee of local landowners. From this emerged the idea of the railway being built by a company funded by the local landowners. The local councils would in turn underwrite the interest payments on the ordinary shares.

Lord Wenlock, and his land agent, Claude Thompson, played a key role in getting things moving. His Lordship had had a distinguished military career after which he was appointed Governor of Madras in India between 1891 and 1896. While there he laid the foundation stone for the Nilgiri Mountain Railway. Returning to the Escrick estate he promoted the DVLR scheme rigorously, making good use of his links with the NER. Other local landowners also wanted a line to be built to transport their goods, and so the idea of a Derwent Valley Light Railway Company (DVLRCo) gained ground.

Therefore, an application was made to the Light Railway Commissioners in May 1905 for the line to be transferred to a limited company constituted for the purpose. That August Lord Wenlock informed the councils that a number of the landowners were also prepared to underwrite half of the councils' potential liability for interest payments. The new LRO was issued on 26 August 1907 transferring the powers to a new company, the DVLRCo. The Company was allowed five years to construct the line, but the Order also stated that any monies given by the councils needed to be repaid in forty years.

Along with Lord Wenlock, who was chairman, the line's first directors were Captain Mervys Dunnington-Jefferson, Claude Thompson, who was appointed managing director, and P.C. Hemmingway. In addition, both local councils had one representative director each. Edgar Ferguson of Chesterfield was appointed engineer for the line. He had recently been involved in the building of the Grassington branch for the Yorkshire Dales Railway. Ferguson began to produce detailed plans for the line early in 1908, although some matters were to change before the line was built.

The Company's capital had been set at £81,000, but there was a long struggle to secure the necessary finance. This included looking at how costs could be reduced, which is probably why Railway No.2, and the triangle at Foss Islands, was never built. However, the Company continued to put on a brave face.

At their meeting of 25 September 1909 the members of Escrick council were informed by the Company that all the arrangements for the construction of the line were now complete.

However, there were clearly more concerns, because on 27 January 1910 the members were read a letter from the Company assuring them that sources of finance were being found, and the line was not being abandoned.

These delays led to the Company seeking a third LRO, which was obtained in May 1910, to extend the time periods to compulsorily purchase land and complete the railway. In fact as late as March 1911 Claude Thompson estimated that they were still £23,500 short of the required amount. This was even though the NER had taken out 5,000 shares in return for a place on the Board. However, by 20 April 1911 Thompson stated that they were now £12,500 short.

The bulk of the new monies received appear to have come from an interesting source. For some years Lord Wenlock had been seeking to sell some of the Escrick estate's paintings to raise money for the line. One painting in particular, of the Duchess of Cumberland by George Romney, led to a dispute as to its ownership resulting in a delay to its potential sale for £10,000. However, it was eventually sold to the London dealers Arthur J. Sulley & Co, the proceeds apparently being used for the purchase of the shares. Therefore, the DVLR can say it was funded by fine art!

Much later the DVLR would feature in another piece of fine art. In the 1950s the artist L.S. Lowry painted the view from Melrosegate bridge looking along the DVLR towards York Minister in his picture 'A view of York'.

With the finance secured the construction of the line between Cliff Common and Skipwith could proceed. Negotiations with the local landowners were started, and the pegging out of the route began in late April 1911.

Construction

On 22 July 1910 Pethick Dix & Co of London had been appointed as contractors for the line, their price of approximately £80,000 being accepted for the work. After all the delays with raising the finance they began work at Cliff Common in May 1911, with apparently no formal 'cutting the first sod' ceremony being arranged.

By this time some changes had been made to the original plans that Ferguson had drawn up. In April 1908 there was a discussion about a new station between the villages of Osbaldwick and Murton, which became Murton Lane station, with the loop that was originally proposed for Osbaldwick being laid there.

Again on the plans a proposed level crossing between Murton Lane and Dunnington was replaced with an overbridge. This had a halt placed beside it that was to become Dunnington Halt. A similar proposal for an overbridge at Wheldrake was abandoned in September 1910. Instead the level of the line was to be raised through a cutting so that it could cross the road, which would be lowered, on a gated level crossing. Meanwhile at Skipwith the station was 'moved' entirely from the south side of the road to the north. This was because of a dispute with the local landowner who wanted the station moved.

As the line passed through a relatively flat landscape there was only one deep cutting on the line at Dunnington, which was to be 21 ft 6 in deep. In addition there were only two overbridges and one underbridge, while the steepest gradient was 1 in 150. This meant the engineering work required was fairly light and so construction could proceed at a reasonable pace,

Above: Presumably taken to celebrate the completion of the DVLR this photograph features the contractor's train at Elvington station, complete with revelers in the open wagons. One suspects that the ladies' light coloured dresses would not have remained clean for long! The locomotive is the contractor's Manning Wardle 'K' class 0-6-0 locomotive, successfully hidden from the bailiffs, while the wagons belong to James Byrom Ltd Contractors of Bury.   (Photo: Hanstock Commercial Postcard)

Left: Some of the original ex-Midland Railway chairs can still be found in use on the revived Derwent Valley Light Railway at Murton Park.   (Photo: J.D. Stockwell)

although negotiations for the purchase of land in York were still taking place.

For the permanent way secondhand 85 lb rail and chairs were purchased from the Midland Railway. These had previously seen service on the Settle and Carlisle line. However, it is interesting that the Board of Trade inspector, in his report before the opening, stated that in places the rail had worn to 80 lb. Today a number of Midland Railway chairs are among the surviving artefacts of the original line.

To assist with the building, the contractors employed a Manning Wardle 0-6-0 class K locomotive of which Pethick and Dix apparently owned three examples. As was usual with these types of railway cash was tight, and during construction contractors often had to get 'creative' in their financial dealings. As a result it was not unknown for the contractors on the Derwent line to play 'hide and seek' between their locomotive and the bailiffs, when

they had problems meeting their financial commitments.

The contractors were not the only ones with financial issues, costs were increasing rapidly. Therefore, in November 1911 an extraordinary DVLRCo shareholders' meeting authorised the issuing of £27,000 worth of 4% debenture stock. This increased the capital of the company to £108,000.

But despite these difficulties by 29 October 1912 progress was sufficiently advanced for the line between Cliff Common and Wheldrake to be opened for freight traffic, which continued while the remaining four and a half miles to Foss Islands were built. Two trains were scheduled to operate each day in the morning and afternoon. In addition the contractor's train was also running, and so 'Staff and Ticket' working was introduced with the sections being Cliff Common to Skipwith; Skipwith to Thorganby and Thorganby to Wheldrake.

In fact, according to the *Yorkshire Gazette* of 19 April 1913, some 6,285 tons of goods were carried on the line between 29 October 1912 and 31 March 1913, along with 45 wagons of livestock. The DVLR hired a locomotive from the NER to operate the freight trains. Opening as far as Elvington had also been considered early in 1913, but the train would only have been able to access the platform.

However, sadly Lord Wenlock, who had strived so hard to ensure the line was built, did not live to see it opened as he had died on 15 January 1912. He had been succeeded as chair of the Board by Lord Deramore, who was to fulfil the role until 1936.

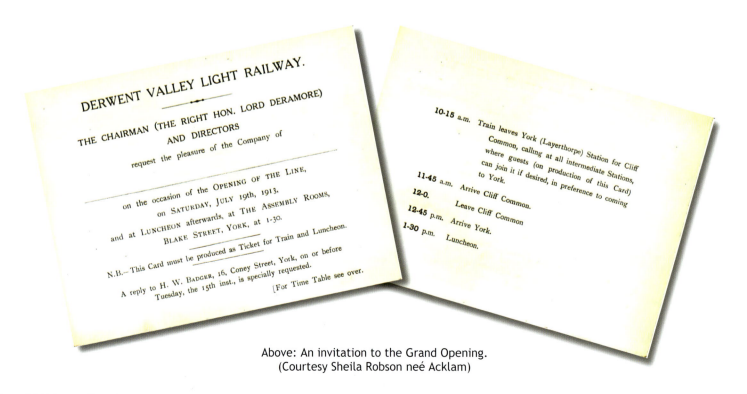

Above: An invitation to the Grand Opening.
(Courtesy Sheila Robson neé Acklam)

Opening

In preparation for the opening of the line an advertisement for a manager appeared in the *Railway Gazette* on 17 May 1912. The person appointed was Mr J.L. Clewes who served the railway between 1912 and 1914, before departing for Ireland.

Gradually progress was being made, although the final parcels of land were still being acquired in late 1912. However, eventually word came the line would soon be ready for opening into York. Therefore, a letter was sent to the Board of Trade on 5 July 1913, requesting an early inspection so that the line could be opened in time for the Yorkshire Show.

The inspection took place on 17 July and Inspector, Lt-Col von Donopand, was happy to pass the line for service utilising the principle of one engine in steam, with three further provisos:

1. Additional ballasting took place where required.
2. That crossing guards and signs were erected at South Moor Lane crossing.
3. A track diagram should be provided in the ground frame hut at Cliff Common.

His permission to open was telegraphed to the Company.

They were doubtless relieved that the formal opening could proceed, as invitations had already been issued for 19 July 1913.

On that day guests assembled at York Layerthorpe station where a special train was due to depart at 10.15 am. The opening ceremony was performed by Lady Deramore, who cut a double blue ribbon which ran from the station building to the locomotive. After the embarkation of the passengers the train departed, fifteen minutes late. In charge of the train was NER locomotive No.1679, a 2-2-4 tank engine, originally built in 1846 as a 2-2-2 tender locomotive, driven by Frank Pickup. This hauled the line's two coaches along with two decorated wagons, each fitted with seats and canvas awnings, and a brake van.

During the journey the train called at intermediate stations, where guests could join the special train. It arrived at Cliff Common at 11.42 am, three minutes early, before returning to York at 12.04 pm arriving there at 12.45 pm.

At all stations, and along the line, it was stated the train was greeted with great jubilation by the local residents, and there was much flag waving by local children. Upon their return to York the guests were then treated to a formal luncheon at the The Assembly Rooms in Blake Street, York.

Above: Lady Deramore cuts the tape at Layerthorpe station on 19 July 1913 to mark the opening of the DVLR.

(Photo: *The York Press*)

Above: A hand-annotated postcard from the DVR archive of part of the opening day party, who rode in the open wagons that had been covered with awnings and decorated for the occasion. Hopefully the benches were fixed to the wagon floor by some means.
(Photo: Hanstock Commercial Postcard)

Above: The scene after the train returns from Cliff Common.   (Photo: *The York Press*)

The Early Years

Above: Original drawing of the station buildings (or mirror image) constructed at Dunnington, Elvington, Wheldrake, Thorganby and Skipwith. Drawing is approximately 3 mm to foot.

Operating the Line

From the start the DVLR had an excellent relationship with the NER, helped no doubt by Lord Wenlock. In 1908 a ten year agreement had been negotiated whereby the NER would supply locomotives and crew for the railway. Later the agreement was changed with the DVLR employing their own crews.

Public passenger services commenced on Monday 21 July 1913, and to convey the anticipated traffic the line had acquired a number of pieces of rolling stock. When the line opened the company owned eight open wagons, two cattle trucks, one brake van, and one hand-operated travelling crane with a match truck. In addition there were the aforementioned two former NER passenger coaches, a third and a brake composite. A third carriage, a composite, was added soon after the line's opening. The coaches initially carried a dark blue livery with gold lettering.

The first passenger service for the summer of 1913 showed four weekday departures from Layerthorpe to Cliff Common at 9.50 am, 2.08 pm, 4.45 pm, 6.33 pm (Monday to Friday to Wheldrake only), and 7.05 pm (Saturdays only to Wheldrake). This timetable allowed between 48 and 53 minutes for the train to run the length of the line. At this point trains were often 'mixed', with goods wagons being attached to the rear of the train and shunted off en-route, while others were added. This of course did not aid timekeeping.

Progress

In just over five months in 1913 a total of 21,692 passengers were carried, which rose to 43,844 in the first full year in 1914. This was helped by the running of a number of excursions to places such as

Bridlington, as well as special services in connection with the Grand Yorkshire Gala.

Of course 1914 also saw the outbreak of World War One, but the DVLR was not taken under the control of the National Railway Executive Committee, being deemed

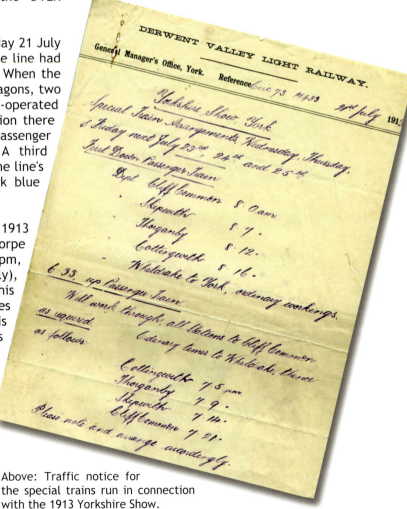

Above: Traffic notice for the special trains run in connection with the 1913 Yorkshire Show.

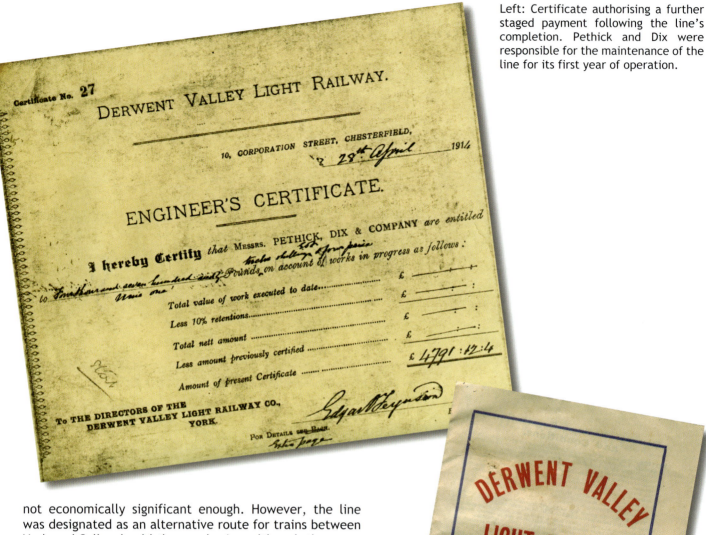

Certificate No. 27

DERWENT VALLEY LIGHT RAILWAY.

10, CORPORATION STREET, CHESTERFIELD,

28th April 1914

ENGINEER'S CERTIFICATE.

I hereby Certify that Messrs. PETHICK, DIX & COMPANY are entitled

to One thousand seven hundred ninety Pounds, on account of works in progress as follows:

Total value of work executed to date.................... £

Less 10% retentions.................... £

Total nett amount .... £

Less amount previously certified .... £

Amount of present Certificate .... £ 1791 : 12 : 4

To THE DIRECTORS OF THE
DERWENT VALLEY LIGHT RAILWAY CO.,
YORK.

For Details see Back.

Left: Certificate authorising a further staged payment following the line's completion. Pethick and Dix were responsible for the maintenance of the line for its first year of operation.

not economically significant enough. However, the line was designated as an alternative route for trains between York and Selby should the need arise, although there are no records of through trains taking advantage of this.

The war did, though, have a positive effect on the railway because the restrictions imposed on fuel etc. limited the development of bus services in the area. As a result the railway's passenger traffic increased, reaching a peak of 49,983 in 1915, before falling back to 46,088 in 1917. There was also a through working to Selby on Mondays for Selby market between 1917 and 1922, with the DVLR's brake van even being inscribed 'For use between Selby and Cliff Common only".

However, by 1914 it was clear that there were further issues the Company needed to face. This was because by the time all the bills had come in for the purchase of land, the construction of the line, and the acquisition of rolling stock as well as other essentials for the operation of the line the total was some £126,000. This was beyond the already authorised capital, and any extra the Company was permitted to raise by the previous LROs. Therefore, a new LRO was authorised in 1915, which granted the Company powers to raise a further £18,000 through new shares. But the LRO stated that these powers were not to be exercised "during the duration of the present war and twelve months thereafter". The company did though obtain permission for £13,000 in 4½% debenture stock to be released in 1918, but the remaining £5,000 was never issued.

DERWENT VALLEY LIGHT RAILWAY.

Via York or Selby.

D V L R

WINTER TIME TABLE

From OCTOBER 1st, 1915, until further notice.

W. T. D. GRUNDY,
General Manager.

YORKSHIRE HERALD CO., LTD., YORK.

Right: A blank free first class pass of the period.

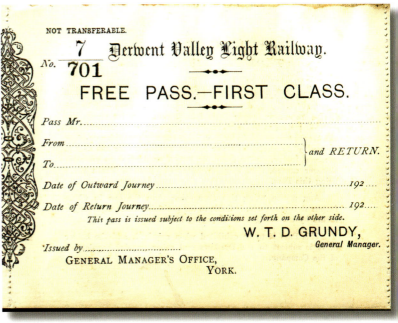

NOT TRANSFERABLE.

No. 7
701

Derwent Valley Light Railway.

FREE PASS.—FIRST CLASS.

Pass Mr...

From...

To... } and RETURN.

Date of Outward Journey.. 192...

Date of Return Journey.. 192...

This pass is issued subject to the conditions set forth on the other side.

W. T. D. GRUNDY,
General Manager.

Issued by..
GENERAL MANAGER'S OFFICE,
YORK.

After the war and the easing of restrictions, there was a small increase in passenger numbers to 47,546 in 1918. However, they fell sharply to 40,459 in 1919 never to recover as increased road competition had more and more effect. This was not helped by the railway deciding to 'upgrade' third class compartments to second class in 1916 with a corresponding fare increase. This was because under the terms of its original LRO it could charge 1d per mile for third class passengers, but 2d per mile for second class, thereby doubling the fares. As this 'upgrading' simply seems to have involved changing the class on the tickets, to say it was unpopular was probably something of an understatement!

Goods, on the other hand, increased across the decade from 18,174 tons in 1913, to 38,620 tons by 1919. Early traffic included potatoes, grain, hay, manure, roadstone and timber. Cattle and other livestock was another important source of traffic, increasing from 1,449 head of cattle being transported in 1913 to a peak, for the entire life of the line, of 7,235 in 1917.

However, there was unrest in the Company. In January 1919 a dispute arose between the DVLR and the National Union of Railwaymen (NUR), over pay; in particular, that the pay-rates on the DVLR had not increased in line with main line workers. This led to a mass meeting of NUR members at York on 26 January when they refused to supply locos for the DVLR.

The situation lasted for three days, and was only resolved when the NER, under government pressure, effectively subsidised a pay increase to the DVLR staff to the tune of

£1,000 per annum until 1921. It is said, though, that during the dispute a petrol tank wagon was hauled by horses along the line from Cliff Common to Layerthorpe, in order to maintain a delivery!

The 1920s

During the 1920s events were reshaping the railways of Britain. Many railways were 'grouped' into the 'Big Four' companies. However, the DVLR, like other Light Railways, maintained its independence. In the early years of the decade passenger traffic continued to decline, and freight tonnages dipped as well. This led to the railway looking for ways to economise.

But in 1923, the year of grouping, the railway's operating agreement with the NER came to an end. Therefore the railway explored the option of acquiring its own motive power, as a means of making savings. To this end the

Left: The original Tang Hall Beck bridge, the only underbridge on the DVLR when it opened. It was converted into a culvert in the late 1920s when the Melrosegate overbridge was built.

(Photo: DVLRS/YMF Archive)

Above: Photograph of the Ford-based railbuses at Layerthorpe station. A copy of this photograph was sent to the Ministry of Transport showing the buses running back-to-back as a single unit. What they failed to mention was that the buses were capable of running independently. Turntables were installed at Layerthorpe and Skipwith to permit this to happen.

(Photo: Rail Archive Stephenson)

railway took delivery of a petrol driven rail locomotive, from the 'British Four-Wheel Drive Tractor Lorry Company' of Slough, for a month's trial. This, as the company name suggests, was essentially a four-wheeled lorry chassis modified to operate on rails with a basic wooden body, in other words a rail-lorry. However, it did not last long, although it made at least two return trips along the whole line, but it was not powerful enough and was unreliable. Consequently the DVLR continued to hire motive power from the NER's successor, the London and North Eastern Railway (LNER).

The Railbuses

Undeterred the Company tried again to obtain new motive power. Therefore in May 1924 the DVLR purchased a pair of Ford petrol railbuses at a cost of £1,070 each. These could carry eighteen passengers each.

They proved to be reasonably successful and reduced the running costs for passenger services to 5d (2p) per mile from 1s 5d (7p), a considerable saving. However, their introduction led to changes having to be made.

Previously the line had always operated on the principle of 'one engine in steam'. Therefore, when the Company tested the rail-lorry, the manager had had to promise the Ministry of Transport (MoT) that the steam locomotive would be 'locked up in sidings'. This meant that, with the railbuses operating the passenger services, while another locomotive was dealing with the goods traffic, different

operating procedures had to be introduced. Therefore, 'Staff and Ticket' working based on four sections from Layerthorpe to Dunnington, Dunnington to Wheldrake, Wheldrake to Skipwith and Skipwith to Cliff Common was proposed.

The new arrangements were inspected and passed by the MoT in August 1924, despite the lack of signals at the loops. There was, though, telephone communication between all stations, which the Inspector considered adequate. This cleared the way for the railbuses to be introduced from November 1924.

However, in December 1924 the MoT noticed that the issued timetable did not correspond with the method of working they had approved. Therefore, they wrote to the railway asking for an explanation. The Company replied the following February explaining that the arrangements had been slightly amended, and included a modified timetable. This included the need to transfer the staff between Skipwith and Cliff Common by bike at one point. But they failed to provide an adequate plan of the new arrangements.

There then followed a series of requests from the MoT for clarification of the situation. These went unanswered, save for one reply from the Company in May 1925, that the manager was away testing a new locomotive (presumably the Sentinel that was purchased). In November 1925 the Company explained the general manager was ill, and the following month they sent

Right: Class J21 No. 1804 at Skipwith in the 1930s. The remains of the railbus turntable can be seen in front of the loco. By this time the siding and running shed had been removed.
(Photo: Lavinia Nelson née Howden)

another plan to the Ministry.

This was immediately returned as not showing the required information. There then followed a long period of silence from the Company, despite regular reminders from the Ministry. They noted that the manager had not personally signed a letter to them for over a year. Finally a letter was sent by Mr Grundy to the MoT on 30 July 1926. This stated that the railbuses had been taken out of service, and the line was now being worked by 'one engine in steam' once more.

It was probably a combination of factors that led to the railbuses' demise. Their introduction does not seem to have arrested the decline in passenger numbers, the 38,373 passengers who travelled on the line in 1920, had become 28,290 by 1923. During 1924, the year the railbuses were introduced, the numbers fell again to 23,344. For 1925 the number was 18,430. Clearly they were not having the desired effect, possibly they were unpopular with passengers due to their rough ride and limited capacity for busy services. However, by now both bus and car competition was a serious threat, it being said that three-quarters of the farmers in the area now owned a car.

In May 1926 the railbuses were lent to the LNER during the General Strike for service between Starbeck and Harrogate, with the operations on the DVLR being suspended. Following their return they were put up for sale in the June and purchased by the County Donegal Railway. In the meantime the passenger service continued, but not for much longer, and an article in the *Yorkshire Gazette*, on 31 July 1926, stated that it was the Company's intention to end passenger services.

The Last Regular Passenger Train

On Tuesday 31 August 1926 the last regular passenger train ran from Layerthorpe to Skipwith. This was powered by the line's Sentinel shunter hauling the line's entire passenger stock. The *Yorkshire Evening Post* recorded that at the end of the journey there were only four passengers, consisting of three journalists and the general manager's wife, the general manager driving the engine.

Passenger numbers had fallen dramatically with only 5,831 travelling since January 1926, and receipts of a meagre £157. It was reported that some trains only had one passenger. On arrival at Skipwith the carriages were shunted into a siding and the passengers returned on the locomotive. However, while it was the end of an era, it was not to be the end of the railway, and even passenger trains in the form of excursions were to return.

More New Motive Power

The DVLR was still anxious to reduce its costs, and so, on 15 June 1925, the magazine *The Locomotive Magazine*

and Railway Carriage and Wagon Review, hereafter referred to as *The Locomotive*, reported that a 20 ton Sentinel steam locomotive had had a trial on the DVLR. This had been attached to a goods train of 220 tons and a LNER dynamometer car. Lord Deramore, Mr Grundy and representatives from the LNER were present for the event, which led to the DVLR purchasing the shunter. The LNER also ordered a number for lighter duties on their lines.

Initially the locomotive seemed to fulfil the needs of the railway, but there were a series of teething problems, which led to it needing repairs, with a replacement steam engine having to be hired in. Nevertheless Lord Deramore, in his address to the DVLRCo's AGM on 18 March 1927, said:
"The Super Sentinel we have in use continues to give economical results and when I inform you that the cost of engine power in 1926 amounted to about £1,200 as against £2,800 in 1924 you will realise that a substantial economy has been affected".

However, the truth was that costs had also been reduced both by the ending of passenger services, and also a drop in freight traffic, from 37,244 tons in 1925 to 29,641 tons in 1926. The railway was now at a low ebb, and a substantial increase in the Company's overdraft to

Above: The Super Sentinel shunter at Layerthorpe shortly after it was purchased in 1925. It is worth noting that at this time the locomotive shed, seen behind the water tower in later photos had not been built, apparently not being constructed until 1928.

(Photo: Rail Archive Stephenson)

£11,859 had to be negotiated at the end of 1926. The coaches were put up for sale, redundancies were made, and the remaining staff went on reduced hours.

At this time there was a change of manager. Mr Grundy departed for the Liverpool Overhead Railway, and Mr S.J. Reading was appointed in his place. He set about building up the links with farmers and traders, as well as seeking to attract new sources of traffic, particularly coal. In this he was successful. However, the Sentinel proved unable to cope with the increased traffic levels, with up to 55 wagons needing to be moved daily. It ended up being sold in early 1929, and the railway returned to hiring locomotives from the LNER, Mr Reading having negotiated a new agreement on reasonable terms. The DVLR would now continue to hire motive power from both from the LNER, and later from British Railways (BR), until the late 1960s.

Under Mr Reading freight traffic on the line continued to increase, reaching 56,446 tons in 1929. This was the highest on the railway since it had opened, and was helped by a bumper potato harvest that year.

There was other traffic as well, at the former Osbaldwick station W. & J. Glossop tar-distillers took over much of the station and yard in 1922. Later National Benzole established a depot at the station in 1927. In 1928 a through LNER cattle train from stations on the Market Weighton line to the York cattle market was run via the

DVLR. Therefore, despite some of the problems of the decade the railway ended it in relatively good shape.

The 1930s

The Wall Street Crash of 1929 led to many railways and businesses struggling with a decrease in trade. On the DVLR, though, there was a relatively stable period in the early 1930s. This was helped between 1931 and 1932 when considerable traffic was carried in connection with the construction of the Osbaldwick electricity sub-station. This amounted to over 3,000 tons with a dedicated siding being laid at the site. One special load was a transformer, which became the largest object ever carried on the DVLR.

At Dunnington station meanwhile a wood yard had been established, and the station yard was occupied from the mid 1930s by Dunn & Co road contractors. All this development meant that the railway carried substantial quantities of freight, with between 50,000 and 60,000 tons being conveyed annually during the 1930s. Not an inconsiderable achievement.

Another change which occurred during this decade happened when Lord Deramore, who had been chairman of the Company since the line opened, passed away. His successor was Claude Thompson, who had been so instrumental in the building of the line. He was to occupy the position for twenty-five years.

Above: Sugar Beet was a major traffic even into the 1960s when this photograph was taken at Elvington station.

(Photo: Transport Treasury)

Part of a copy of the *Derwent Farmers' News* from February 1934.

Relationships with Farmers

As the farming community was very much the raison d'être for the existence of the DVLR, it was important that the Company maintained good relationships with them; therefore, Mr Reading went to agricultural shows and met with the farmers listening to their requirements. As a result a number of new ideas were tried.

These included the DVLR offering farmers the option of wagons being left on the line overnight, at convenient places between stations for loading or unloading. Farmers could also stack potatoes on the lineside to be loaded onto trains, which would stop as needed for the purpose. Sugar beet had become an increasingly important crop in the area, and so extra sidings were installed at Broad Highway in 1927, as well as Sledmere crossing in 1928.

The railway also produced a pamphlet called the *Derwent Farmers' News*. This was delivered free to local farms every month from February 1932 up until January 1940. It contained information about general farming matters, as well as the special facilities the DVLR had to offer. For example, from 1933 the newsletter contained the information that the DVLR had now started running the Monday cattle train directly to Foss Islands market.

Another innovation offered to farmers from 1927 were delivery and collection services, which were based on Layerthorpe and Elvington stations. In 1932, to encourage more traffic, rates for agricultural produce were reduced. In addition, free delivery was offered on five ton loads of oil cake feed. Post Office telephones had also been installed at all DVLR stations so that orders, collections and deliveries could be arranged directly.

A further example of this co-operation was the contract between the railway and the garrison at Catterick for the supply of manure. The railway did this because the change from horse-drawn to mechanised transport created a shortage of manure for the farmers. Therefore,

as horses were still based at the garrison and produced copious supplies of the commodity, the railway undertook to remove it, and sell it to the local farmers at cost price.

Accidents

The first known accident on the DVLR occurred on 8 October 1913 when a platelayer, F. Pullen, had had to have his hand amputated after it was run over by a reversing locomotive in Layerthorpe yard. An official report was prepared into the accident. In it the Board of Trade Inspector recommended that tender locomotives should no longer be used on the line. This was due to the restricted vision the crew had when running tender first. Therefore, tank locomotives took over operations on the line, although tender engines were to reappear later.

In 1937 there were two fatal accidents at crossings. The first occurred on 5 July at one of the occupation crossings just west of Osbaldwick station. A lorry, which had been delivering gravel for the new sewerage works on the north side of the line, collided with a locomotive hauling a cattle wagon and guards van. The lorry driver, John Lamb, was killed.

At the inquest which followed, witnesses stated that the locomotive whistled while approaching the crossing, but Mr Lamb appeared not to notice it. The verdict was accidental death.

Just over a month later, on 11 August 1937, another fatal crash occurred. Mrs Edith Cape and her daughter, Elizabeth, of Thorganby Hall, were killed after being thrown from their car following a collision at Cottingwith station. This occurred at about 4 pm, when the car Elizabeth was driving was hit by the daily pick-up goods returning from Cliff Common. Mrs Cape died instantly, but her daughter lingered for several days, before succumbing to her injuries.

There appear to be no formal MoT reports on either of these later incidents. But newspaper articles from March 1938 state that the railway and local authorities, after consultation with the Ministry, had installed improved warning signs at the DVLR crossings.

Left: LNER class N12 0-6-2 tank locomotive No.2486, built in 1901 is seen at Elvington in the early 1930s. Also worthy of note in this photo is the National Benzole tank wagon being transported from the firm's depot at Osbaldwick.
(Photo: J.K. Perkin
Copyright J.B. Perkin)

The Second World War and Beyond

Without doubt World War Two had a profound effect on the DVLR. The railway not only had to cope with carrying increasing agricultural traffic, but also had to do its bit for the war effort.

As in World War One the railway was not taken under government control, but fearing for its financial future it petitioned the MoT to do so. This was particularly because the two petroleum depots had been closed on the outbreak of war, with an estimated loss to the DVLR of £2,500 per year. A question was even asked in the House of Commons by Col. William Carver M.P. for Howdenshire, who was concerned that the line might have to close.

Mr Reading wrote to the Ministry about how the railway might serve several purposes during the war. He said that it could act as a diversionary route, or as a means of evacuating the city of York. In addition, there were two warehouses that were available to store potatoes, and also there were storage and distribution facilities for foodstuffs. Finally, he stated, there was the option to build storage depots on railway land. But the MoT, clearly anxious not to be taking on what might be a 'lame duck' with little strategic importance even as a diversionary route, declined.

However, it was at this point that the railway's poor finances, and lack of maintenance, came to its rescue. When the RAF took aerial photographs of the line it could not be seen due to its overgrown state. Therefore, the Company was told not to weed the line, so it would remain invisible to the enemy, and its strategic importance rose significantly. The DVLR had become a stealth railway!

Along the line various new depots and other facilities were opened. Murton Lane station yard was requisitioned by the War Department, and was known as the Northern Command Petrol Depot. Large numbers of cans of petrol and oil were stored in the yard and surrounding fields. In 1943 105 special trains were worked for this traffic. In one 24 hour period just before D-Day, no fewer than 100 wagon-loads were dealt with. However, the railway was warned off from advertising the presence of the depot. There was a request from the Ministry that the 1941 AGM should be postponed to prevent any unnecessary publicity. They also stated that the postponement should not be advertised either!

One of the main sources of traffic was construction materials for Elvington and Riccall aerodromes, where work began in 1941. When it opened in October 1942, Elvington was home to No.77 Squadron and their Halifax bombers. Later, in May 1944, it became the base of the Free French Air Force. As a result the main traffic through Elvington station yard became bombs and ammunition, with an extra siding being laid for the purpose. In addition, a nearby brickyard building was converted into a storage depot for tea by the Ministry of Food. This also produced significant amounts of traffic on the railway.

At Skipwith station yard construction materials for Riccall aerodrome had been dealt with until it opened in September 1942. This included the construction of a tarmacadam plant. When it opened the aerodrome became the heavy conversion station for No.4 Group of Bomber Command. Skipwith continued to handle supplies for the station, including bombs and ammunition.

In July 1942 an ordnance depot was constructed at Layerthorpe. This was used for storing imported Ford engines and spares, and had its own dedicated siding. Towards the end of the war Layerthorpe also became a railhead for aviation fuel used by planes at Linton and Full Sutton aerodromes.

Meanwhile at Wheldrake, land was requisitioned for use as a bomb storage area. Wheldrake also handled considerable quantities of petroleum in tank wagons destined for Melbourne airfield. This was for their fog-dispersal system known as FIDO which will be described later.

Above: Some of the Italian POWs and locals at Skipwith. Stationmaster Henry Howden is seated third from the left with Ned Jackson to his left. (Photo: Lavinia Nelson)

Left: Changing of the guard at Layerthorpe. On 20 January 1967 the ex-SECR six-wheel brake stands nearest the camera with the ex-LNER four-wheel pigeon brake, which had been bought to replace it, behind.
(Photo: R.R. Darsley)

More controversially at Cottingwith a mustard gas storage depot was established in June 1944 at a cost of £99,000. It was on twenty acres of land requisitioned for the purpose, and linked by a siding to the DVLR. Again the details of this depot will be given later.

All this extra activity led to increased maintenance for the permanent way being necessary. Therefore, Italian prisoners of war were brought in to work as platelayers. From May 1944 twenty POW's were employed at Layerthorpe, and, the following month, twenty at the Cliff Common end. The latter being based at Skipwith. They were considered hard working, and when one POW was moved to another camp, he would leave the camp without breakfast in order not to be late for work. Some of the POWs were even invited to local homes for Sunday lunch.

It is important not to forget as well the contribution from the farmers to the war effort. The drive to increase home food production led to increasing tonnages of crops being carried. For example, in 1938 2,363 tons of potatoes had been transported on the DVLR. In 1942 there were 8,785 tons of potatoes carried, along with 4,677 tons of sugar beet, 11,812 tons of grain and other produce. In addition, 3,056 head of cattle were transported that year. There was also 33,616 tons of coal and coke, 45,320 tons of stone, 3,990 tons of oil, 42,064 tons of spirit liquids, and 1,448 tons of timber. All this activity ensured that the railway made a profit through most of the war years, even paying its first dividend since 1923 in 1941.

There was also representation from the local community for passenger services to be resumed. This was following the withdrawal of local bus services. However, the level of agricultural and government traffic flowing along the line, meant there was not sufficient capacity for passenger operations to be resumed.

Due to its 'camouflage' the DVLR escaped major bomb damage. However, on the night of 24 September 1942 two incendiary bombs were dropped on the line at Tang Hall, but they caused relatively minor damage.

Post-World War Two and Nationalisation

After the war the DVLR acquired what became its most iconic piece of rolling stock, the former South Eastern and Chatham Railway (SECR) six-wheeled passenger brake van with its distinctive birdcage lookout. This was purchased from the Southern Railway in 1946 to replace a former NER brake van. The brake van was often used by enthusiasts visiting the line in the post-war period, and was frequently photographed by them.

As far as the general fortunes of the line were concerned, there was a gradual reduction in the traffic associated with the facilities built for the war effort. But new industries began to take their place. In 1947, for example, a depot for breaking up or repairing old railway wagons was established at Murton Lane. This generated significant traffic for the railway, and a similar facility was developed at Elvington.

The same year also saw new coal storage facilities with concrete pens built in station yards down the line. Garages for the coal merchants' lorries were also provided at Layerthorpe. One of the harshest winters on record also occurred that year, with one guard disappearing up to his neck in a snow drift when he stepped down from his train. Snow drifts prevented trains running the length of the line for six weeks. Nevertheless the Company recorded net revenue for the year of £3,888. However, over a quarter of its income came from property rents rather than the operation of the railway.

Of course what was dominating the railway world at that time was the subject of nationalisation, which leads to

Above: Class J25 No.65687, ex-LNER No.2048 built in 1899, stands at Cliff Common with the daily freight on 9 May 1953. As can be seen from the make up of the train with tank, covered and open wagons, a wide variety of goods are being carried. Almost towering over the locos are the piles of timber which were stored along the line as part of a government scheme.

(Photo: C.H.A. Townley Copyright Industrial Railway Society)

the question as to why the DVLR wasn't nationalised? This is particularly apposite, as it was felt that many minor railways would be left 'high and dry' if they were not taken over by the government. The matter was taken up with the MoT by the Association of Minor Railways at a meeting on 20 December 1946. At this the reply was that "a line had to be drawn somewhere". It seems that, in major part, this line was based on those railways that had come under government control during the wars. This is why some railways, such as the DVLR and the Talyllyn, slipped through the net.

A further deputation from the DVLR went to the Ministry on 24 February 1947. This consisted of Mr Thompson as chairman, Mr Forbes-Adam one of the directors, Mr Reading as general manager and Mr Harland as company solicitor. They put forward four reasons why the line should be nationalised. These were, that it was standard gauge; carried essential goods; could provide an alternative to heavily loaded routes, and was an integral part of the main line system. However, the Ministry were not to be swayed.

But in the end it is probably true that the DVLR would not have lasted as long as it did had it become part of the nationalised system. As doubtless it would have been closed, along with many other branch lines, in the wake of the Beeching Report. Indeed it could be said that the DVLR became an alternative model for what could have been done with some of the secondary lines. However,

this would have depended on there being a more creative approach to generating traffic and other income.

The 1950s

During the 1950s more changes came to the line. In the late 1940s the government decided to stockpile timber, and the DVLR was chosen as it was able to offer a number of storage locations in the station yards along the route. Therefore, large quantities of timber began arriving on the railway, and were piled at various points along the line by workers brought in from Hull docks. Extra land was even purchased, or leased, as required. This was to last until the policy was reversed in 1959, but it explains why large timber stacks are to be seen in many photographs of the period.

In 1952 a site at Wheldrake station was chosen by the Ministry of Works for a 'buffer' depot, to store foodstuffs in the event of nuclear war. Following the construction of the warehouse, large supplies of sugar, as well as other commodities, were received and sent out by rail.

Another development occurred at Dunnington in 1955. Here a grain drying plant was built by Yorkshire Grain Driers Ltd, on land sold to the firm by the DVLR. Grain from the locality was brought to the plant to be dried, ready to be transported by rail to distilleries in Scotland. Initially the grain was handled in sacks, but bulk grain wagons were used from 1958.

Left: A Branch Line Society excursion, hauled by class J21 No.65064, pauses at Skipwith on its way to Cliff Common on 17 May 1958. (Photo: D.A. Kelso)

Meanwhile at Osbaldwick in 1959 the station yard was leased to a ready-mixed cement company, Site Supply and Excavation Ltd. Despite these developments freight traffic fell, from 93,922 tons in 1950 to 63,880 tons in 1953. It was to remain around 60,000 tons annually until the end of the decade.

However, Claude Thompson, as chairman of the Board remained optimistic. At the 1957 AGM he was able to state that the railway had made a small profit in 1956, and that sugar beet and petroleum traffic had increased. Similarly at the 1958 meeting he reported that receipts for 1957 amounted to £24,216, with an expenditure of £21,886, so that the railway remained in profit. The railway also continued to be able to support a 5% dividend to shareholders for this period.

One developing source of traffic during the 1950s was visiting rail enthusiasts. Some of these came as individuals and rode in the 'birdcage' brake van. Others came as part of organised railtours which visited the line during the 1950s and subsequently. These will be dealt with later.

The 1960s

The 1960s saw major changes to the DVLR, starting with the motive power employed on the line. After the war ex-LNER J25s had been the mainstay of the line with the occasional J21 being used on specials. However, by 1961 it was proving difficult for BR to supply an appropriate steam locomotive. Therefore, class 03 diesels were used. Another change came in 1961 when Lt-Col Sir John Alexander Dunnington-Jefferson succeeded Claude Thompson as chairman of the Company. Meanwhile Mr Reading retired in 1963, with Mr Acklam taking up the position of general manager.

Closure from Wheldrake to Cliff Common

However, the general fortunes of the railway were not going well. A small operating profit for the railway in 1960 of £1,036, became an operating loss of £2,442 in 1963, followed by one of £2,844 in 1964. Despite this the Company did continue to make a profit due to its properties. Part of the losses was stated to be due to a reduction of coal traffic while a new mechanised coal plant was built at Layerthorpe. This was opened on 12 October 1964, and was capable of handling 40,000 tons of coal a year, all brought in by rail by BR for distribution in the locality.

At this point events elsewhere had also had an effect on the DVLR. The Beeching cuts led to the announcement of the closure of the Selby to Market Weighton line, with Cliff Common being closed for goods in January 1964. This was nearly a decade after the passenger service was withdrawn, although the line itself remained open until the summer of 1965. On the DVLR the southern section of the line was already lightly used and losing money. Therefore, in July 1964 the Board announced that it would close the line between Wheldrake and Cliff Common. This would reduce the length of the line to just under nine and a half miles. Staff levels could also be reduced with the track and land being sold off.

No objections were received to the Board's application for the abandonment order, and so plans for closure proceeded, the order being made on 9 February 1965. In the meantime news about the proposed closure had spread. This resulted in the Railway Correspondence and Travel Society (RCTS) organising special trains over the line from Layerthorpe to Cliff common and return. These ran on consecutive Saturdays 9 and 16 January 1965. Soon afterwards contractors Marple and Gillott of Sheffield started dismantling the track.

Above: The first of the RCTS specials to mark the closure of the line between Wheldrake and Cliff Common at Skipwith on 9 January 1965 with class 03 D2111 in charge.
(Photo: G. Morrison)

Above: The final passenger train prepares to depart from Layerthorpe to Cliff Common on 16 January 1965 again with D2111 heading the train.
(Photo: *The York Press*)

A Changing Emphasis

Above: DVR locomotive No.2 in Layerthorpe yard with some bulk grain wagons on 18 May 1977. The coal depot can be seen behind the wagons.
(Photo: David J. Mitchell)

With the closure of the southern section, and the new coal plant at Layerthorpe, the Company's fortunes improved. At the AGM in April 1966 it was reported that the railway had made a small operating profit of £378, with the Company making an overall profit of £5,720. In addition £14,175 had been made by the sale of the track on the abandoned section. Freight tonnage had increased again with 77,651 tons being conveyed along the truncated route in 1965.

However, there was one announcement at the meeting that really foreshadowed a major change in the nature of the Company. As will have been seen already, at this point the Company made more money out of its property portfolio than railway operations. There now came an announcement that the Company had purchased land at Elvington for £2,251, which would be let to Agriform Fertilisers Ltd. From now on property was going to play an increasingly important role in the Company, with the railway becoming more and more secondary. A subsequent acquisition saw ten acres of land at Dunnington purchased for industrial development.

In October 1966 Agriform fertilisers opened their depot at Elvington station, but unfortunately the bulk of the fertilizer traffic arrived and departed by road. On 15 July 1967 Layerthorpe engine shed was seriously damaged by fire. This included BR Drewry shunter D2113, which was inside at the time. Happily not only was the locomotive repaired, but it has now been preserved by the Heritage Shunters Trust.

Another section of the line closed in 1968. The *Yorkshire Evening Post* reported on the last train to run between Wheldrake and Elvington on 14 May, driven by William Watson. The line was not, though, officially abandoned until the 24 May. However, despite the closures, traffic had increased on the line over the decade. In 1969 although 80,402 tons were carried, the railway made an operating loss of £1,234.

In spite of this the DVLR made the bold move to purchase a pair of Drewry class 04 0-6-0 diesel shunters from BR in 1969. Ex-D2298 came from Gateshead to become DVLR No.1, while ex-D2245 from Goole became DVLR No.2. They were painted in the silver-grey livery seen above.

One interesting 'might-have been' for the DVLR was a request discussed at a meeting held on 29 April 1969. Present at the time were representatives of the Company and the Blue Peter Locomotive Society. Under discussion was a request by the Blue Peter Society to run steam services on the DVLR in the summer months. This would not have involved the *Blue Peter* itself, as it was still undergoing restoration at the time. Unfortunately the DVLR could not agree to a regular service, but would

Right: The locomotive shed at Layerthorpe on 20 January 1967. This was severely damaged by fire a few months later and subsequently replaced.
(Photo: R.R. Darsley)

agree to a three day steam event over the August Bank Holiday, between Layerthorpe and Dunnington. In the end, though, this did not take place.

The 1970s

The beginning of a new decade saw a new chairman for the railway with Lt-Col Dunnington-Jefferson retiring after 54 years on the Board. He was replaced by Roy Cook, who was also managing director of Yorkshire Grain Driers at Dunnington, and was to take the Company into a new era. Part of this was the preparation of the site at Dunnington for development, which included laying two replacement sidings and removing the old loading dock. Meanwhile the purchase of the two locomotives, plus a third for spares, meant that the locomotive and maintenance facilities at Layerthorpe had to be extended and improved during 1970.

However, in the annual report for 1971 major changes were foreshadowed, despite the railway making an increased operating profit of £3,717. First there was concern over the effect of the miners' strike in the early months of 1972, which it was felt would certainly affect revenues and profits. Secondly there was the need to upgrade the permanent way at Layerthorpe. Here improvements to the fuel depot were being made, so that 100 ton bogie tank wagons could be dealt with.

As a result a full assessment of all the railway's permanent way was undertaken. Much of this still dated back to the opening of the line nearly sixty years previously. Therefore, the decision was taken to relay the yard at Layerthorpe, and the main line towards Dunnington using concrete sleepers where necessary, the first phase of which it was estimated would cost £14,000 in 1972.

This involved relaying the main line through Layerthorpe with 95 lb bullhead rail, and concrete sleepers, to one

hundred yards beyond the sidings. The purpose of the latter was to act as a shunting neck for the bogie tank wagons. In addition, the two sidings serving the oil depot were relaid. As a further measure spot re-sleepering took place between Sledmere crossing and Dunnington bridge. However, it was also decided to close the line between Dunnington and Elvington, as it was not economic to renew the track on this section.

There is some confusion as to when the section between Dunnington and Elvington officially closed. The abandonment order was signed on 28 December 1972, but it is reported that the last train ran on 22 June that year. Meanwhile the Annual Report for 1972 stated that the track had been sold during the year, raising the sum of £10,020, and the land was under offer. However, it was decided to retain the Elvington station site, as it still brought in a good income from the industries based there.

Another blow to the railway came when it was announced that British Sugar Corporation's York refinery would no longer be accepting sugar beet by rail after 1972. This brought to an end the last staple source of agricultural traffic on the line, other than the products of the grain driers at Dunnington. In addition, other potential sources of traffic, such as the transport of shale to Murton Lane for use on the construction of the York by-pass, did not materialise. This would have seen class 37 diesels running up to six trains a day along the line.

Of course the 1970s were years of economic upheaval, due to factors such as the Middle East oil crisis, much industrial unrest and increased inflation. The railway was also committed to improving the permanent way to the point where the line could be rated for 20 ton axle loadings throughout. Previously the line had been upgraded to 15 tons in 1914, and then to 17 tons in 1938.

However, this came at a cost of £30,000 between 1977

Above: Hardwicke returns from Dunnington approaching Melrosegate bridge on 12 April 1977 as part of the specials run for Yorkshire Television. It was this section of track that was subject to continuing trespass, and acts of vandalism, from the 1920s through to the closure of the line. (Photo: B. Myland)

and 1978, and actually only involved the complete relaying of half a mile of track from Layerthorpe towards Osbaldwick. Meanwhile sleepers salvaged from the relayed section were used to reinforce track joints along the rest of the line.

In Layerthorpe yard two sidings were removed to reduce the number of facing points, and facing point locks required for the proposed new passenger excursions. Changes also took place at Dunnington, where the long siding was shortened and the spur siding to the old loading dock removed. The line was, however, upgraded for 20 ton axle loadings at a speed of 10mph from the summer of 1978.

The concern of the Company that they should be seen as a 'proper' railway also led them to abandon the word 'Light' from the Company title, becoming the Derwent Valley Railway (DVR) from 23 March 1973. However, there was another development in the middle years of the decade, which was to lead to the regular re-introduction of passenger services on the railway. The meeting of the Blue Peter Locomotive Society has already been mentioned, but in 1973 there was an approach from Flying Scotsman Enterprises about running excursions on the line, involving *Flying Scotsman* itself. However, the state of the track precluded the use of any heavy steam locomotive on the line.

Nevertheless exploration of the possibility of operating a regular steam service continued. This was boosted after some passenger services were run in conjunction with the Friends of the National Railway Museum (NRM), using the Museum's *Hardwicke* locomotive on 9 October 1976. As a result it was decided to introduce a regular steam hauled service between Layerthorpe and Dunnington in 1977. For this the DVR obtained the services of class J72 0-6-0 tank locomotive *Joem*, along with three ex-BR Mark One coaches. Services were run from the summer of 1977, but only lasted until 1979.

Interestingly in 1977 the DVR also carried out a survey of local people, in conjunction with North Yorkshire County Council, to see if a 'Park and Ride' service at Dunnington at peak times to and from York was viable. This would have used a locomotive and single carriage, and would also have served Rowntree Halt on the Foss Islands branch. Sadly there was insufficient support.

In May 1978 the DVR sold diesel shunter No.2 to the Shackerstone Railway. It was replaced by a Fowler 0-4-0 diesel mechanical purchased from the British Pipe Line Agency at a cost of £1,127. It was painted in green and named *Claude Thompson*. Meanwhile DVR No.1 had also been repainted in green (reminiscent of NER livery) and named *Lord Wenlock*.

Above: *Joem*, seemingly in need of a clean, waits at Layerthorpe with one of the steam specials. It is worth noting that by this time the main line through Layerthorpe, to the left of *Joem*, has been relaid with concrete sleepers.   (Photo: T. Heavyside)

Closure

By now the railway was beginning to steadily lose money, although the property interests were bringing in around £20,000 per year. Other factors also began to have an effect, the decline in the coal market led to the closure of the coal depot at Layerthorpe in August 1980. Meanwhile the tonnages of grain carried also declined. This was in spite of a contract being won in 1979 for grain to be sent to Moray Firth Maltings in Inverness. For this the DVR chartered wagons from Procor UK, the first time the DVR had provided wagons to run over BR metals.

Finally the inevitable decision was made to close the railway operation, and the last freight train to Dunnington ran on Tuesday 22 September 1981. On Sunday 27 September 1981 the last train ran over the DVR between Layerthorpe and Dunnington. This was organised by the British Rail Staff Society using DVR No.1 *Lord Wenlock* and four Mark One coaches hired from BR for the event.

The train was well advertised with tickets sold at £5 for adults and £2.50 for children. Enthusiasts came from all over the country to travel on the last train, which was well-loaded for the journey, with others photographing it as it went past.

This was not, though, the last movements on DVR metals. The Shell-BP depot continued to be used after the line to Dunnington closed, with the remains of the DVR track being used for access. These movements lasted until October 1988, but as we shall see they were still not destined to be the last trains along the route of the DVLR.

It was not the end either for the DVR company as it still continued to operate its profitable property portfolio, and remained listed on the London Stock Exchange. It sponsored a Bill through Parliament to allow it to repay the original debenture stock, the £40,000 necessary coming from the sale of the track and other equipment from the railway. These, along with the station buildings, cottages and unwanted land, raised a total of £150,000. Layerthorpe yard itself became the Ebor Industrial Estate, plus a DIY warehouse and garden centre. Part of the route also became a cycle path.

In 1985 the Derwent Valley Railway Company was reconstituted as Derwent Valley Holdings plc, and was effectively taken over to be used to develop a London based property business by John Burns, and his partner Simon Silver. It is now known as Derwent London, and is still a successful enterprise. Ironically, in 1986 the remaining railway operation of a few hundred yards of track made a profit of £17,000, a figure previous generations could only have dreamed of!

Above: Last days at Dunnington as DVR No.1 *Lord Wenlock* and Yorkshire Grain Driers' *Churchill* are seen shunting on 16 September 1981.

(Photo: David J. Mitchell)

Above: The DVR Farewell special with DVR No.1 *Lord Wenlock* about to pass under Melrosegate bridge, as it returns to Layerthorpe on 27 September 1981. Jim Acklam, the DVR's last general manager, appears to be leaning out of the cab on this side.

(Photo: R. Patrick)

Right: DVR No. 1 returns to Layerthorpe light engine having passed under Dunnington bridge on 16 September 1981. By this time the track is nearly overgrown.

Below: The same view in March 1982 after the track had been lifted.

(Both Photos: David J. Mitchell)

Right: The final section of the DVR to survive is seen here as class 08 diesel shunter No.08771 shunts some oil tankers out of Layerthorpe yard, on the left, and onto the Foss Islands branch on 2 July 1987.
(Photo: Duncan McEvoy)

Passenger Operations

Above: The earliest known photograph of an ordinary passenger train on the DVLR taken at Cliff Common in the summer of 1913 and seems to feature the line's two original carriages.   (Photo: Courtesy *The Railway Magazine* October 1913)

There were a number of distinct phases to passenger operations on the DVLR. The first was the regular service operated between 1913 and 1926. Following this there was then a period up until World War Two when the DVLR organised its own special excursion trains. After the war a new type of passenger traffic came on the scene, the rail enthusiast, with both individuals and small groups riding in the railway's brake van. There were also larger railtours which visited the line. Finally in the late 1970s the DVR operated its own steam hauled services in the summer season, before the final excursions were arranged to mark the line's closure.

The Initial Passenger Service

The first passenger timetable is shown below:

PROVISIONAL TIMETABLE JULY TO SEPTEMBER 1913

WEEKDAYS UP	a.m.	p.m.	p.m.	p.m. SX	p.m. SO
York (Layerthorpe)	9.50	2.08	4.45	6.33	7.05
Osbaldwick	9.55	2.13	4.50	6.38	7.10
Murton Lane	9.58	2.16	4.53	6.41	7.13
Dunnington Halt	10.02	2.20	4.57	6.45	7.17
Dunnington	10.06	2.24	5.01	6.49	7.21
Elvington	10.12	2.30	5.07	6.55	7.27
Wheldrake	10.18	2.36	5.13	a7.01	a7.33
Cottingwith	10.22	2.40	5.17		
Thorganby	10.26	2.44	5.21		
Skipwith and North Duffield	10.31	2.49	5.26		
Cliff Common	a10.38	a2.56	a5.33		
Cliff Common (NER)	10.49	3.08			
Selby (NER)	10.57	3.14			

WEEKDAYS DOWN	a.m. TSO	a.m.	a.m.	p.m.	p.m. SX	p.m. SO
Selby (NER)				3.40		
Cliff Common (NER)			10.49	3.47		
Cliff Common (DVLR)	8.00		11.00	3.50	5.40	6.10
Skipwith and North Duffield	8.07		11.07	3.57	5.47	6.17
Thorganby	8.13		11.12	4.02	5.52	6.22
Cottingwith	8.16		11.17	4.06	5.56	6.26
Wheldrake	a8.20	8.25	11.21	4.10	6.00	6.30
Elvington		8.31	11.27	4.16	6.06	6.36
Dunnington		8.37	11.33	4.23	6.12	6.42
Dunnington Halt		8.41	11.37	4.26	6.16	6.46
Murton Lane		8.46	11.43	4.31	6.21	6.51
Osbaldwick		8.49	11.46	4.34	6.24	6.54
York (Layerthorpe)		a8.53	a11.50	a4.38	a6.28	a6.58

SO - Saturday Only   SX - Saturday Excepted   TSO - Thursdays and Saturdays Only   a - Arrival time

There were never any regular timetabled trains on the line on Sundays until the 1970s steam revival. Thursdays and Saturdays were market days in York. Special third class market day tickets were available priced 1s 8d from Cliff Common, with similar reduced fares being offered from other stations. Another interesting aspect at this time is the advertised free luggage allowance, which was 120 lb for first class passengers, and 60 lb for third class.

From 1 October 1913 a new winter timetable operated, with an increased time allowed for the full journey of between 55 and 60 minutes. The following summer more changes were made as seen in the timetables below:

It has to be said that the timetables seem complex for what was a fairly basic operation. By the winter timetable of 1915 there were further changes, including more trains originating and terminating at Skipwith. Osbaldwick had also been closed as a passenger station. This permitted the fastest journey time to be reduced to 50 minutes for the full length of the line, although many trains were timetabled for longer, presumably in part to allow for shunting.

The winter timetable of 1919 and the summer of 1920 had a couple of curiosities. First was that the 12.30 pm train from Layerthorpe was only timetabled to run to

TIMETABLE OCTOBER 1913 TO MARCH 1914

WEEKDAYS UP	a.m.	p.m.	p.m.	WEEKDAYS DOWN	a.m. TSO	a.m.	a.m.	p.m.
York (Layerthorpe)	9.40	12.50	5.25	*Selby (NER)*				*3.40*
Osbaldwick	9.45	12.55	5.30	*Cliff Common (NER)*			*10.49*	*3.47*
Murton Lane	9.48	12.58	5.34	Cliff Common (DVLR)	8.15		11.00	4.00
Dunnington Halt	9.52	1.02	5.38	Skipwith and North Duffield	8.23		11.09	4.09
Dunnington	9.57	1.07	5.44	Thorganby	8.29		11.16	4.16
Elvington	10.05	1.15	5.52	Cottingwith	8.33		11.20	4.20
Wheldrake	10.12	1.22	6.00	Wheldrake	a8.40	8.45	11.27	4.27
Cottingwith	10.16	1.26	6.04	Elvington		8.52	11.35	4.35
Thorganby	10.21	1.31	6.09	Dunnington		9.00	11.43	4.43
Skipwith and North Duffield	10.26	1.36	6.16	Dunnington Halt		9.04	11.48	4.48
Cliff Common	a10.35	a1.45	a6.25	Murton Lane		9.08	11.52	4.52
Cliff Common (NER)	*10.49*		*6.36*	Osbaldwick		9.11	11.55	4.55
Selby (NER)	*10.57*		*6.45*	York (Layerthorpe)		a9.15	a12.00	a5.00
TSO - Thursday and Saturday Only				a - Arrival time				

TIMETABLE APRIL TO SEPTEMBER 1914

WEEKDAYS UP	a.m. MSX	a.m. MSO	p.m WSX	p.m. WSO	p.m. SO	p.m. SX	p.m.	WEEKDAYS DOWN	a.m.	a.m. SO	a.m.	p.m. SO	p.m. SX	p.m.
York (Layerthorpe)	9.20	9.40	1.00	1.50	4.25	5.15	7.05	*Selby (NER)*			10.18		3.40	4.55
Osbaldwick	9.25	9.45	1.05	1.55	4.30	5.20	7.10	*Cliff Common (NER)*			10.25		3.47	5.02
Murton Lane	9.28	9.49	1.08	1.59	4.34	5.23	7.13	Cliff Common (DVLR)		8.15	11.00	3.15	3.55	s6.00
Dunnington Halt	9.32	9.53	1.12	2.03	4.38	5.27	7.17	Skipwith and North Duffield	T8.00	8.24	11.09	3.24	4.04	6.10
Dunnington	9.37	9.59	1.17	2.09	4.44	5.32	7.22	Thorganby	T8.06	8.31	11.16	3.29	4.09	6.15
Elvington	9.44	10.07	1.24	2.17	4.52	5.39	7.29	Cottingwith	T8.10	8.35	11.20	3.34	4.14	6.20
Wheldrake	9.52	10.15	1.32	2.25	5.00	5.47	a7.37	Wheldrake	8.15	8.41	11.27	3.38	4.18	6.24
Cottingwith	9.56	10.19	1.36	2.29	5.04	5.51		Elvington	8.22	8.49	11.35	3.45	4.25	6.31
Thorganby	10.01	10.24	1.41	2.34	5.09	5.56		Dunnington	8.29	8.57	11.43	3.53	4.33	6.39
Skipwith and North Duffield	10.06	10.31	1.46	2.41	5.16	a6.01		Dunnington Halt	8.33	9.02	11.48	3.58	4.38	6.44
Cliff Common	a10.15	a10.40	a1.55	a2.50	a5.25			Murton Lane	8.37	9.06	11.52	4.02	4.42	6.48
Cliff Common (NER)	*10.49*	*10.49*		*3.08*	*6.36*			Osbaldwick	8.40	9.10	11.55	4.05	4.45	6.51
Selby (NER)	*10.57*	*10.57*		*3.14*	*6.45*			York (Layerthorpe)	a8.45	a9.15	a12.00	a4.10	a4.50	a6.56

MSX - Mondays and Saturdays Excepted   MSO - Mondays and Saturdays Only   WSX - Wednesdays and Saturdays Excepted
WSO - Wednesdays and Saturdays Only   SO - Saturdays Only   SX - Saturdays Excepted   T - Thursdays Only
s - Ran to Cliff Common Saturday only   a - Arrival time

TIMETABLE FROM OCTOBER 1915

WEEKDAYS UP	a.m. A	p.m. SX	p.m. SO	p.m. SO	p.m. SX	p.m. SO	WEEKDAYS DOWN	a.m.	a.m.	p.m. SO	p.m. SX	p.m. SO
York (Layerthorpe)	9.30	12.50	1.20	4.20	5.50	6.10	Selby (NER)		10.18	1.18	3.40	
Murton Lane	9.36	12.56	1.26	4.26	5.56	6.16	Cliff Common (NER)		10.25	1.25	3.47	
Dunnington Halt	9.39	12.59	1.29	4.29	5.59	6.19	Cliff Common (DVLR)		11.00	3.00	4.15	
Dunnington	9.44	1.04	1.40	4.34	6.04	6.24	Skipwith and North Duffield	8.00	11.10	3.10	4.25	5.20
Elvington	9.50	1.10	1.50	4.40	6.10	6.30	Thorganby	8.05	11.15	3.15	4.30	5.25
Wheldrake	9.57	1.17	2.05	4.47	6.17	a6.37	Cottingwith	8.10	11.20	3.20	4.35	5.30
Cottingwith	10.00	1.20	2.08	4.50	6.20		Wheldrake	8.13	11.23	3.23	4.38	5.33
Thorganby	10.05	1.25	2.15	4.55	6.25		Elvington	8.20	11.30	3.30	4.45	5.40
Skipwith and North Duffield	10.10	a1.30	2.25	a5.00	a6.30		Dunnington	8.26	11.36	3.36	4.51	5.46
Cliff Common	a10.20		a2.50				Dunnington Halt	8.31	11.41	3.41	4.56	5.51
Cliff Common (NER)	10.49		3.08				Murton Lane	8.34	11.44	3.44	4.59	5.54
Selby (NER)	10.57		3.14				York (Layerthorpe)	a8.40	a12.00	a4.00	a5.20	a6.00

A- Ran ten minutes later on Mondays   SX - Saturday Excepted   SO - Saturday Only
a - Arrival time

Wheldrake, but was permitted to run through to Cliff Common for parties of ten or more by arrangement. It would be interesting to know if this facility was ever used. The second oddity was the 3 pm Saturdays only from Cliff Common, which only stopped at intermediate stations to pick up passengers for York, and set down passengers from Cliff Common. It had a journey time of 45 minutes, the fastest ever timetabled on the DVLR.

Another item in the timetable was that on Mondays the 10.20 am arrival at Cliff Common was effectively 'hired' by the NER to form the 10.30 am train to Selby, to serve the market there. This arrangement started on 5 March 1917 and lasted until 10 July 1922. Between January 1918 and March 1919 the DVLR train was also used to form a return working from Selby at 4.20 pm, with the DVLR receiving 7s 6d (37.5p) from the NER for each train run.

The next major change was the introduction of the railbuses on 17 November 1924. These were based at Skipwith. The first train of the day was driven up to Layerthorpe by Henry Howden, the porter-in-charge, who

TIMETABLE FROM 1 JUNE 1920

WEEKDAYS UP	a.m.	p.m. SX	p.m. SO	p.m. SO	p.m. SX	p.m. SO	WEEKDAYS DOWN	a.m.	a.m. MSX	a.m. MSO	p.m. SO	p.m. SX	p.m. SO	p.m. SO
York (Layerthorpe)	9.20	12.30	1.20	4.20	6.00	6.30	Selby (NER)							
Murton Lane	9.26	12.36	1.26	4.26	6.06	6.36	Cliff Common (NER)							
Dunnington Halt	9.29	12.39	1.29	4.29	6.09	6.39	Cliff Common (DVLR)			10.50	3.00			
Dunnington	9.32	12.42	1.32	4.32	6.12	6.42	Skipwith and North Duffield	7.50	10.20	11.00	B	6.45	5.05	7.34
Elvington	9.38	12.48	1.45	4.38	6.18	6.48	Thorganby	7.54	10.24	11.04	B	6.49	5.09	7.38
Wheldrake	9.45	12.55	1.57	4.45	6.25	6.55	Cottingwith	7.58	10.28	11.08	B	6.53	5.13	7.42
Cottingwith	9.48	C	2.00	4.48	6.28	6.58	Wheldrake	8.01	10.31	11.11	B	6.56	5.16	7.45
Thorganby	9.52	C	2.04	4.52	6.32	7.02	Elvington	8.08	10.38	11.18	B	7.03	5.23	7.52
Skipwith and North Duffield	9.56	C	2.08	a4.56	a6.36	a7.06	Dunnington	8.14	10.44	11.24	B	7.09	5.29	7.58
Cliff Common	MSa10.06	C	a2.18				Dunnington Halt	8.17	10.47	11.27	B	7.12	5.32	8.01
Cliff Common (NER)	T10.30						Murton Lane	8.20	10.50	11.30	B	7.15	5.35	8.04
Selby (NER)	T10.36						York (Layerthorpe)	a8.26	a10.56	a11.40	a3.45	a7.20	a5.41	a8.10

MSX-Mondays and Saturdays Excepted   MSO - Mondays and Saturdays Only
MS - Only ran to Cliff Common on Mondays and Saturdays   B - Stopped if required to pick up for York or set down from Cliff Common   C - Ran to Cliff Common for parties of ten or more by arrangement   T - Through service to Selby on Mondays
SO - Saturdays Only   SX - Saturdays Excepted   a - Arrival time

TIMETABLE FROM 17 NOVEMBER 1924

WEEKDAYS UP

WEEKDAYS UP	a.m.	p.m.	p.m. SO	p.m. SO	p.m.
York (Layerthorpe)	8.45	12.30	1.20	4.00	6.00
Murton Lane	8.52	12.37	1.27	4.07	6.07
Dunnington Halt	8.56	12.41	1.31	4.11	6.11
Dunnington	9.00	12.45	1.35	4.15	6.15
Elvington	9.07	SX12.52	1.42	4.22	6.22
Wheldrake	9.15	SX1.00	1.50	4.30	6.30
Cottingwith	9.19	SX1.04	1.54	4.34	6.34
Thorganby	9.24	SX1.09	1.59	4.39	6.39
Skipwith and North Duffield	9.31	SXa1.16	a2.06	a4.46	a6.46
Cliff Common	Ma9.40				
Cliff Common (NER)	M9.56				
Selby (NER)	M10.04				

WEEKDAYS DOWN

WEEKDAYS DOWN	a.m.	a.m. SO	a.m. MSX	a.m. MO	a.m. SO	p.m. SO	p.m. SO	p.m. MO	p.m. MX
Selby (NER)								4.05	
Cliff Common (NER)									
Cliff Common (DVLR)				9.50				4.15	
Skipwith and North Duffield	7.45		9.45	10.01	11.00		2.25	4.26	5.00
Thorganby	7.50		9.50	10.06	11.04		2.30	4.34	5.05
Cottingwith	7.55		9.55	10.11	11.08		2.35	4.36	5.10
Wheldrake	7.59		9.59	10.15	11.11		2.39	4.40	5.14
Elvington	8.07		10.07	10.23	11.18		2.47	4.48	5.22
Dunnington	8.14		10.14	10.30	11.24	12.50	2.54	4.55	5.29
Dunnington Halt	8.18	10.00	10.18	10.34	11.27	12.54	2.58	4.59	5.33
Murton Lane	8.22	10.04	10.22	10.38	11.30	12.58	3.02	5.03	5.37
York (Layerthorpe)	a8.31	a10.11	a10.31	a10.47	a11.40	a1.05	a3.11	a5.12	a5.46

MSX-Mondays and Saturdays Excepted   MO - Mondays Only   M - Only runs to Cliff Common on Mondays
MX - Mondays Excepted   SO - Saturdays Only   SX - Saturdays Excepted   a - Arrival time

would then return with his brother, Raymond Howden, the regular driver. A similar arrangement in reverse allowed Henry Howden to bring the railbuses back to Skipwith for the night.

The introduction of the railbuses seems to have encouraged Mr Grundy to introduce some extra short run trains on Saturdays (see timetable above). These did not last long as a revised timetable was introduced the following February (see below) with these services removed. In both versions of the timetable the 11 am

departure from Skipwith on Saturdays was a mixed steam working, with the engine arriving via Cliff Common. The fact that the train was not timetabled to run from Cliff Common indicates that the coaches were also stabled at Skipwith. After this the steam locomotive then worked the daily 1.30 pm goods departure from Layerthorpe, presumably returning the carriages to their base in the process on Saturdays.

Even with declining passenger numbers due to road competition, some of the services could be popular,

TIMETABLE FROM FEBRUARY 1925

WEEKDAYS UP

WEEKDAYS UP	a.m.	p.m.	p.m. SX	p.m. SO	p.m. SO
York (Layerthorpe)	8.45	12.30	1.20	4.00	6.00
Murton Lane	8.52	12.37	1.27	4.07	6.07
Dunnington Halt	8.56	12.41	1.31	4.11	6.11
Dunnington	9.00	12.45	1.35	4.15	6.15
Elvington	9.07	12.52	1.42	4.22	6.22
Wheldrake	9.15	1.00	1.50	4.30	6.30
Cottingwith	9.19	1.04	1.54	4.34	6.34
Thorganby	9.24	1.09	1.59	4.39	6.39
Skipwith and North Duffield	9.31	1.16	a2.06	a4.46	a6.46
Cliff Common	Ma9.40	Ma1.25			
Cliff Common (NER)	M9.56				
Selby (NER)	M10.04				

WEEKDAYS DOWN

WEEKDAYS DOWN	a.m.	a.m. MSX	a.m. MO	a.m. SO	p.m. SO	p.m. MO	p.m. MX
Selby (NER)						4.05	
Cliff Common (NER)							
Cliff Common (DVLR)			9.50			4.15	
Skipwith and North Duffield	7.45	9.45	10.01	11.00	2.25	4.26	5.00
Thorganby	7.50	9.50	10.06	11.04	2.30	4.34	5.05
Cottingwith	7.55	9.55	10.11	11.08	2.35	4.36	5.10
Wheldrake	7.59	9.59	10.15	11.11	2.39	4.40	5.14
Elvington	8.07	10.07	10.23	11.18	2.47	4.48	5.22
Dunnington	8.14	10.14	10.30	11.24	2.54	4.55	5.29
Dunnington Halt	8.18	10.18	10.34	11.27	2.58	4.59	5.33
Murton Lane	8.22	10.22	10.38	11.30	3.02	5.03	5.37
York (Layerthorpe)	a8.31	a10.31	a10.47	a11.40	a3.11	a5.12	a5.46

MSX-Mondays and Saturdays Excepted   MO - Mondays Only   M - Only runs to Cliff Common on Mondays
MX - Mondays Excepted   SO - Saturdays Only   SX - Saturdays Excepted   a - Arrival time

Left: A photograph of the Sentinel on a passenger train at Layerthorpe. This was probably taken in the summer of 1926 after the railbuses had been sold.
(Photo: Courtesy *The Railway Magazine* August 1927)

especially the 6 pm departure from Layerthorpe on a Saturday evening. Often a run to Murton Lane was made before the railbuses returned to pick up the passengers for the rest of the line. Even then driver Howden remembered squeezing sixty-plus people into the two vehicles, which had been designed for a total of thirty-six.

The latter timetable apparently lasted right through to the end of regular passengers services, not changing even after the railbuses had been disposed of. On 31 August 1926 the last train was the 6 pm departure from Layerthorpe, with the Sentinel locomotive returning light engine from Skipwith with those who had travelled to record the last train.

Excursions

Pre-World War Two

While regular passenger services may have ended in 1926, this was far from the end of passenger trains on the DVLR. As early as July 1913, only days after the line was formally opened, special trains were run to the Yorkshire Show in York between 23 and 25 July. This was part of the reason for the directors' desire to get the line open. These were achieved by starting the first train of the day from Cliff Common instead of Wheldrake at 8 am, and the last train being extended to Cliff Common arriving at 7.21 pm.

In 1914 a number of excursions and special workings operated. These included, excursions to the Grand Yorkshire Gala between 17 and 19 June. There was also an excursion from Elvington to Bridlington on 1 July, which involved the use of two NER carriages. On 28 July there was an excursion between Wheldrake and Bridlington. Later, on 30 July, the scheduled late return of an NER excursion between Cliff Common and

Instructions for special workings in connection with the Grand Yorkshire Gala in June 1914.

Brough for a 'Conservative Demonstration', meant that a late evening train ran from Cliff Common at 10.05 pm arriving at Layerthorpe at 11 pm. Where NER carriages were hired for these services they were supplied at a daily charge of 4s (20p) for six-wheelers, or 7s 6d (37.5p) for bogie stock. Another condition was that they could only access DVLR metals via Cliff Common.

Later excursions were run to Harrogate for the Royal Show in 1929 with passengers being transferred from Layerthorpe station to the main LNER station by bus. They then had reserved seats on the 9.40 am special train to Harrogate which returned at 6.10 pm. It is recorded that over eighty passengers were carried.

There was another excursion to the Yorkshire Show in Leeds in 1932, which was advertised in the *Yorkshire Herald* of 13 June 1932 as follows:

'The DVL Railway announce that they propose to run an excursion in conjunction with the L & NE railway company ... to the Yorkshire show in Leeds on July 13th, provided a guaranteed number of passengers can be obtained. Exceptionally low fares are quoted ....the fare may be paid on the instalment plan in four weekly payments'

The last mentioned facility was certainly an innovative form of marketing. Other pre-war excursions were run to Scarborough on 31 July 1936, and to Whitley Bay in July 1938.

Meanwhile back in 1928 there was pressure from York residents for trains out to Skipwith. This led to the running of three excursions on Bank Holiday Monday 6 August from Layerthorpe. These then became the 'Blackberry Specials', which started on Saturday 8 September. These departed from Layerthorpe at 1.45 pm and returned from Skipwith starting at 7.20 pm. In total the trains carried 1,916 passengers during the year. The excursions attracted wide attention with an article even appearing in *The Daily Chronicle*. As a result the railway was often known as 'The Blackberry Line'. On 21 September 1928 the *Leeds Mercury* reported one of these outings:

'Passengers carried all kinds of bags, baskets and tins.... even buckets! Alighting at Skipwith the party split into two sections. The stationmaster's wife led one party down the line, and the stationmaster himself directed

Working instructions for excursion to Bridlington 1 July 1914.

Left: An excursion party at Skipwith station possibly off to the seaside judging from the buckets and spades some of the children are holding.
(Photographer Unknown Courtesy The North Duffield Conservation and Local History Group)

Above: On 27 April 1954 the Imperial College Railway Society rode the daily goods train from Layerthorpe to Cliff Common, which is seen at the latter station with class J25 No.65677 waiting to start the return trip. Obviously someone has chalked on an unofficial headboard. Later the secretary of the Society wrote to thank the Company for their hospitality.

(Photo: J.J. Davies Copyright Historical Model Railway Society)

the others to the best areas for blackberries.

Six hours later, when we returned to the station, every basket, tin - and bucket - was full.

The stationmaster, of course, is delighted with the resumption of passenger traffic… He acts as signalman, telegraphist, crossing keeper, and booking clerk, and warns passengers of the approaching danger of fire on the common at the same time as he collects their tickets. "Next season we shall cater for more holidaymakers", I was told "A special train can be obtained for a party of 25 and upwards … people do not need to be millionaires to get a 'special'". Eight 'Blackberry Specials' have been run already, carrying about 1,000 people to Skipwith, Thorganby, Cottingwith and Wheldrake'.

By this time the DVLR had sold their own coaches, and so LNER carriages had to be hired in for these trains. Nevertheless they obviously proved profitable and these special trips and excursions for various parties continued into the 1930s. A York resident, Beryl Brooke, recalls one Sunday School outing:

'We went to Layerthorpe station and went by train to Wheldrake, where we played games in the field and had a picnic and then returned home'.

Post-World War Two

As stated previously, in the 1950s a number of enthusiasts visited the line and were allowed to travel as passengers in the ex-South Eastern and Chatham Railway (SECR) six-wheel brake van on the daily freight trains. The

decreasing cost of photography meant that many pictures were taken during these trips.

In addition to these visits the DVLR began to welcome enthusiast specials. On Sunday 20 June 1954 the first recorded Sunday passenger train ran on the DVLR, when an RCTS organised special travelled the length of the line from Cliff Common to Layerthorpe. The train consisted of six bogie coaches hauled by class J21 0-6-0 tender locomotive No.65078 with 250 enthusiasts on board. This event was even mentioned in the *Daily Mail*.

A later excursion on 7 April 1956 consisted simply of one coach on the daily goods train, with class J25 0-6-0 tender locomotive No.65714. On 17 May 1958 there was a special organised by the Branch Line Society worked by class J21 0-6-0 tender locomotive No.65064. This train ran from Layerthorpe to Cliff Common, with the return journey being made non-stop. This was possibly the first 'express' passenger service over the whole line.

The biggest excursion ran on 27 September 1963, being organised jointly by the RCTS and Stephenson Locomotive Society (SLS). This was part of a five day trip covering 1,100 miles all over the North East. Starting from the main York station, the train joined the DVLR at Layerthorpe and then ran to Cliff Common, before going on to Selby. It was hauled over the DVLR by ex-LMS Ivatt 2-6-0 No.46409, of which we will be seeing more later. Following this there were the previously mentioned specials in January 1965 in connection with the closure of

Above: On 7 April 1956 an excursion took place with BR class J25 No.65714 hauling a single coach along the line with the daily goods working. The train is seen at Thorganby en-route to Cliff Common. (Photo: J.C. Halliday)

the line to Cliff Common.

Even the end of steam on the line did not finish the specials. One little-known excursion occurred on 14 May 1966. This was a train organised for a party of BR employees belonging to the British Railways (Eastleigh) Engineering Society. It consisted of one coach hauled by BR class 03 D2075 and ran from Layerthorpe Station to Wheldrake and back. Later on 6 January 1973 a five coach train was worked down the DVLR using the railway's class 04 diesel shunters in each direction between Layerthorpe and Dunnington. About 230 enthusiasts took part in the trip, which was organised by the Locomotive Club of Great Britain (LCGB), and originated from Warrington. But there was even more excitement when the return of steam to the line was proposed.

Steam Revival

Following the opening of the National Railway Museum (NRM) in 1975, York was becoming even more popular as a tourist destination. Therefore, the DVR directors considered the possibility of running steam specials over the line. At the time there was considerable concern about the state of the permanent way, and so the size of locomotive, as well as the number of trips that could be worked were limited. On 16 September 1976 a special train hauled by the NRM's *Hardwicke*, an ex-LNWR Precedent class 2-4-0 tender locomotive, ran over the DVR using the NRM's *Duke of Sutherland's saloon*. This was for the DVR directors, along with invited guests from British Rail and the NRM, to ride as a test run for the proposed excursions.

Right: A group from the Wakefield Model Railway Society prepare to ride the train from Layerthorpe on 4 August 1959.
(Photo: R. Redman)

Right: *Hardwicke* with the *Duke of Sutherland* saloon at Layerthorpe on 16 September 1976. This was for the special test run in preparation for the later excursions, and subsequent regular steam service.
(Photo: *The York Press*)

This must have been a success as on 9 October 1976 *Hardwicke* was used on a number of public specials. These ran between Layerthorpe and Dunnington with *Hardwicke* hauling three BR Mark One coaches. Passengers paid £1.85 for the 75 minute round trip. As previously mentioned, at the time there were even some thoughts of a steam 'park and ride' scheme into the main York station. Consideration was also given to a new recreational and picnic facility beside the by-pass at Osbaldwick.

After this Yorkshire Television (YTV) ran a special with *Hardwicke* over the DVLR from York, via the Foss Islands branch, on 12 April 1977. The train making a couple of return trips between Layerthorpe and Dunnington for filming. It is understood that YTV chartered the service to make a documentary about a former DVLR employee who lived at Osbaldwick.

With these successes behind them, the DVR decided to introduce a regular steam hauled tourist train in the summer of 1977. This was after further track improvements had taken place. These included the removal of sidings at Layerthorpe to reduce the number of facing points, and hence point locks required, for the running of passenger trains.

To operate the service, the DVR initially hired, and later purchased, former LNER/BR class J72 0-6-0 tank No.69023 *Joem* from the Ainsworth family. The preserved locomotive had been based on the Keighley and Worth Valley Railway, but latterly was stored at Embsay on the Yorkshire Dales Railway, before arriving at Layerthorpe in February 1977.

Left: *Hardwicke* is reflected in a pool of water as it departs from Layerthorpe on 9 October 1976 with one of the experimental passenger services.
(Photo: R. Wildsmith)

Above: *Joem* at Layerthorpe on 18 May 1977 a fortnight after the first of the regular revived services ran. A skeleton staff helped run the train with the general manager's son-in-law acting as guard on occasions, while the station staff at Layerthorpe had to drive to Dunnington in order to serve refreshments when the train got there. There was also a mobile crossing keeper who drove ahead to open the gates for the train as it passed down the line.   (Photo: David J. Mitchell)

Services commenced on 4 May 1977 with invited guests and the Lord Mayor of York, Cllr J. Archer, present. A special gold coloured ticket was produced for the occasion. Trains then ran Tuesday to Sunday departing Layerthorpe at 2.30 pm and returning at 4 pm, the fare being 85p. The trains proved popular with over 10,000 passengers travelling between 4 May and 2 October when the service ended. The KWVR's *Old Gentleman's* saloon, then on loan to the NRM, was also used for passengers paying a supplement. Occasionally a couple of grain wagons were attached to the return working!

Encouraged by these results the DVR even ran Santa Specials in December 1977. The steam trains ran again from 1 May 1978, Sundays to Fridays, with the fare now £1.00 for adults. Passengers could also charter their own train in the mornings or evenings for a minimum £100 charge. Once again Santa Specials were run in the December.

These, however, proved less successful and, with increasing costs, the Company decided in the spring of 1979 that the services would end on 31 August 1979. This was despite a free bus service being offered between the NRM and Layerthorpe via York station. The services having run on Tuesdays, Wednesdays, Thursdays and Fridays from 5 June 1979.

A final farewell trip was organised by the Friends of the National Railway Museum. This ran on Sunday 25 November 1979, consisting of J72 *Joem* and three Mark One coaches hired from BR for the occasion. The original DVR Mark Ones having been sold to the North Yorkshire Moors Railway in the meantime. *Joem* was sold back to the Ainsworth family, and was subsequently bought by the North Eastern Locomotive Preservation Group.

As a postscript to this; the chairman made a comment, in the DVR Annual Report for 1979, that the sale of the equipment had made sufficient to cover the losses the services had made over the three years. Once more the DVR's business sense had made the best of the situation!

Of course the last train to run on the DVR between Layerthorpe and Dunnington was an enthusiasts' special, as already recorded. It is also pleasing to note that, at the time of writing, *Joem* is due to return to the DVLR for the centenary celebrations in July 2013.

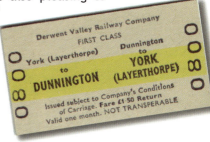

Above: *Joem* is seen returning from Dunnington with its train including the KWVR's *Old Gentleman's* saloon, which is ex-NER saloon No.1661 built in 1904, and is of course famous for its appearance in the film *The Railway Children*. The train is approaching Melrosegate bridge on the approach to Layerthorpe station. (Photo: T. Heavyside)

Above: *Joem* arrives at Dunnington with its train on 12 June 1977 when its was sporting a special headboard to celebrate the Queen's Silver Jubilee. (Photo: T. Heavyside)

Above: A classic view of *Joem* by the buffer stops at Dunnington, as seen from the other side of the former level crossing on 18 May 1977. Probably one of the issues that led to declining numbers for the steam trips was that Dunnington provided little by way of being a 'destination', other than what the railway laid on.
(Photo: David J. Mitchell)

Above: *Joem* prepares to depart from Dunnington on 18 May 1977.
(Photo: David J. Mitchell)

Left: On the last day of the DVR's steam operation, 25 November 1979, two trains were run. The first of these was to celebrate the National Traction Engine Club's Silver Jubilee. *Joem* is seen passing the remains of Murton Lane station with this train, on what was to be its last day of operation on DVR metals until 2013.   (Photo: P. Rounce)

Right: A week before the final closure the DVR directors hired a Diesel Multiple Unit for one last run along the line. This took place on 25 September 1981. The train is seen here approaching Osbaldwick Road crossing. DVR driver Ken Bell is acting as 'pilot' in the cab's second seat.
(Photo: Stephen Chapman)

Left: The last train on the DVR waits to return to Layerthorpe on 27 September 1981.
(Photo: R. Patrick)

Goods Operations

Above: BR diesel D2112 stands at Layerthorpe ready to set out with the daily goods train on 21 July 1964 (This type of locomotive was later designated as class 03). At this time agricultural traffic was low, and there were no grain wagons in the train, but there is one 'Presflo' cement wagon as well as the ubiquitous ex-SECR brake. D2112 has been preserved and is currently based at the Rother Valley Railway.
(Photo: David J. Mitchell)

Information on the DVLR's goods services is somewhat more scarce than the passenger operations, this being particularly true for after the latter ceased. As a result, most of our knowledge comes from the observations of visiting enthusiasts, who rode the trains by special permission. Nevertheless we do have the initial timetable for services between Cliff Common and Wheldrake from 29 October 1912. These were as follows:

GOODS WORKINGS FROM 29 OCTOBER 1912

UP	a.m.	p.m.	DOWN	a.m.	p.m.
Wheldrake	9.30	4.05	Cliff Common	8.20	2.55
Thorganby	s	4.25	Skipwith and North Duffield	8.40	s
Skipwith and North Duffield	s	4.40	Thorganby	8.55	s
Cliff Common	9.50	4.50	Wheldrake	9.05	3.35
s - shunts if required					

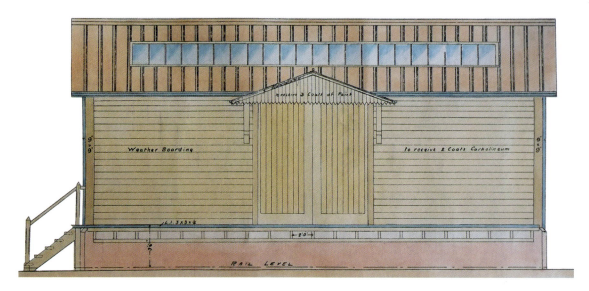

Above: Original drawing of the track side of the goods sheds at Elvington and Wheldrake, reproduced at approximately 3mm to the foot.

When the railway was operating passenger services, the goods workings had to be timetabled around them and also maintain the principle of one engine in steam on the line. From October 1913 the goods services consisted of a weekday working from Layerthorpe to Cliff Common at 6.30 am arriving at 7.55 am. This delivered empty wagons that had been ordered by stations, as well as any inward wagons from the NER at Layerthorpe. There was then an 8.15 am working (mixed on Thursdays and Saturdays) to Wheldrake, conveying up to ten wagons for Elvington and stations to Layerthorpe, which became the 8.45 am mixed working from Wheldrake.

Wagons were then attached to passenger trains as required until 1.50 pm when there was a dedicated goods train between Cliff Common and Dunnington, returning from Dunnington at 2.55 pm, and shunting the stations en-route as required before arriving back at Cliff Common at 3.50 pm. After this wagons were again attached to the passenger services as required.

In April 1914 there was an early morning train from Layerthorpe at 7 am which proceeded as far as Wheldrake, except on Thursdays when it ran to Skipwith, and Saturdays when it went through to Cliff Common. Then in the afternoon there was a light engine working from Cliff Common at 2.05 pm to shunt stations as required, before returning to Cliff Common at 3.40 pm with any remaining wagons. Inward wagons from York via Layerthorpe were then attached to any convenient passenger service, while inward wagons via Cliff Common were added to the 11 am passenger working from that

Above: A view of the track side of the goods shed at Wheldrake, which can be compared with the drawing above.
(Photo: K. Nelson)

Left: Unloading tank wagons in Layerthorpe yard in 1935. One wagon is being discharged into the road tanker via a bottom outlet. The person on top of the wagon is presumably watching the fuel level drop.
(Photo: Ronald Shephard Courtesy West Sussex Record Office)

Right: Another photo taken in 1935 showing the unloading gantries for pumping out the fuel from top discharge tank wagons at Layerthorpe. Also worthy of note are the coal wagons on their 'standings' on the left, which would be unloaded by the coal merchants ready for deliveries in the locality.
(Photo: Ronald Shephard Courtesy West Sussex Record Office)

Left: During World War Two the DVLR handled considerable quantities of petroleum products. This is illustrated here by this train of tank wagons seen at Osbaldwick in 1942.
(Photo: Ronald Shephard Courtesy West Sussex Record Office)

Left: Cattle were an important traffic on the line, given that the station at Layerthorpe was adjacent to York cattle market, and so the DVLR owned a number of their own cattle wagons. This photograph was taken in 1943.
(Photo: Ronald Shephard DVRCo Archive)

station. Outward bound wagons could be dispatched via Cliff Common attached to the 1.50 pm train, or through Layerthorpe by the 3.55 pm working from Cliff Common (3.15 pm on Saturdays).

This was probably the pattern of services through most of the early years of the line, with the single steam locomotive hauling both goods and passenger trains, many of which were mixed. However, with the coming of the railbuses in 1924 a different pattern of working emerged. Now from the 17 November timetable there was a single daily goods train working across the middle of the day. It departed from Cliff Common at 10 am on Mondays to Fridays, and arriving at Layerthorpe at 12.15 pm passing the railbuses at Skipwith as it did so, before returning at 1.30 pm.

However, on Saturdays it worked as a mixed train from Skipwith at 11 am arriving at Layerthorpe at 11.40 am. It then returned to Cliff Common at 1.30 pm, passing the railbuses at Wheldrake en-route, and arriving at Cliff Common at 3.30 pm. This was achieved by the introduction of 'Staff and Ticket' working, to enable both the goods trains and passenger services to run at the same time. But, as mentioned previously, the Inspector was unhappy that the staff sections, and particularly which points the staffs operated, did not match with the approval given, and hence their inquiry of December 1924.

Mr Grundy then modified the timetable in February 1925. Now the goods train departed from Cliff Common at 10 am Monday to Friday, and 11 am on Saturdays but no longer formed a mixed train. The train arrived at Layerthorpe at 12.15 pm and 11.40 am respectively and no longer crossing the railbuses en-route. It then returned at 1.30 pm, crossing the railbuses at Wheldrake on Saturdays, before arriving at Cliff Common at 3.30 pm.

However, there is likely to have been a change in the goods train timings from mid-1925 when the railway's Sentinel shunter arrived. This was based at Layerthorpe, and probably led to the early morning goods train being reinstated. An indication of this is given by a memo from Mr Grundy that, from Monday 25 January 1926, the early morning goods train must depart from Layerthorpe at 6.30 am promptly in order to cross the railbuses at Dunnington. It also stated that a new working timetable would be issued shortly. Therefore, it seems as if he had changed the timetable again. This could be part of the explanation as to why the Ministry of Transport got no answer to their repeated requests for information on the staff sections.

With the end of passenger services in 1926, the line again reverted to the principle of 'one engine in steam'. By August 1928 there was a daily goods train running the length of the line picking up and setting down wagons as required. This seems to have been the pattern for much of the life of the railway, except for special trains being organised for specific traffic, such as occurred at the potato or sugar beet harvest. On 28 April 1938, for example, it is recorded that 181 tons of potatoes were loaded in twenty hours from Wheldrake to Goole bound for Spain, with 34 wagons being used for the task. As already mentioned, one of the innovations that Mr Reading brought in, was to permit wagons to be left on the line to be loaded or unloaded, and then collected when the train passed by again.

During the 1920s and 1930s the majority of trains were made up of open wagons, which were suitable to deal with the traffic of the time such as coal, timber, potatoes etc. There is though, at least one photograph of a LNER *Quint* bogie bolster wagon at Dunnington in the 1920s. One major load that was transported on the line was a transformer that was destined for the new electricity

Above: The largest load ever conveyed on the DVLR was this transformer being delivered to the new sub-station at Metcalfe Lane Crossing, Osbaldwick, in 1931.
(Photo: *The York Press*)

Above: An unknown N12 class 0-6-2 at Wheldrake station on 28 April 1938 with a train of potatoes bound for Spain via Goole docks.
(Photo: *The York Press*)

Left: The daily pick-up goods ridden by the Wakefield Railfans on Wednesday 22 November 1961, which, as can be seen, was a very misty day. The train is pictured at Elvington.

(Photo: J.W. Holroyd)

Right: Loading sugar beet at Skipwith on 22 November 1961.

(Photo: J.W. Holroyd)

sub-station near Osbaldwick in 1931 using bolster wagons.

The DVLR owned only a small amount of rolling stock. Therefore the majority of wagons came from other companies, mainly the NER, or its successor the LNER, but also from the London Midland and Scottish Railway (LMS), and a wide variety of private owners such as from the South Yorkshire collieries. Increasing amounts of petroleum products were also transported up and down the line in tank wagons.

It was World War Two that was to have a significant effect on the traffic carried on the line. Certainly given the amount of goods transported to and from the various depots on the line, during the latter stages of the conflict in particular, it is reasonable to speculate that there was some relaxation of the 'one engine in steam rule'. There is reference to the LNER providing additional locomotives during those years, and one suspects that the national emergency would have taken preference over regulations. How this was done is a matter of conjecture, perhaps a return to the staff sections abandoned in the 1920s.

After the war, and into the 1950s, changes in the traffic handled led to changes in the make up of the daily trains. Now there were more covered vans, as things such as

foodstuffs were delivered to the depots on the line. Later the building of the grain drying facility at Dunnington led to bulk grain carriers being seen on the trains from 1958. Cement also began to arrive on the railway destined for the plant at Osbaldwick in 'Presflo' wagons.

In around 1960 it was reported that the daily train departed Layerthorpe at 10.30 am. A visit by the Wakefield Railfans on Wednesday 22 November 1961 gives a flavour of the line at this time. The following is based on a combination of the accounts of this visit by John Holroyd and Michael Bradley:

'It was a typical November morning … foggy. We caught the 9.10 am 'North Briton' Leeds to York …. From Layerthorpe we rode in the six-wheel SECR brake van hauled by 03 D2103 with six empty mineral wagons and a covered van, the train being delayed waiting for a delivery of parcels from British Railways before departing at 11.23 am.
Depending on whether sidings were trailing or facing the train would drop or pick up wagons on either the outward or return journey. At one place a wagon was left on the main line … this was propelled to the next facing siding for collection on the return journey. The wagon was full of sugar beet and an empty wagon had been left in its place. By the time the train reached Elvington at 12.25

Above: Both of the DVR's diesels can be seen in action at Dunnington on 17 November 1972. One is shunting a load of wagons filled with sugar beet, while the other is dealing with some bulk grain wagons. (Photo: R.R. Darsley)

the train had picked up three wagons loaded with sugar beet.

Elvington was the lunch break. We found a platelayer's trolley and in John's words "we kept ourselves warm pumping up and down the track". Meanwhile the loco had picked up another wagon of sugar beet before departing at 1.22 pm.

Wheldrake was reached at 1.35 pm, and we had time to walk back and photograph the only signal on the line, while another wagon of sugar beet was added to the train. Thorganby was reached at 1.55 pm, a very busy stop, the station building is in good condition, but the clock had stopped. Skipwith was passed at 2.05 pm. Arrival at Cliff Common was at 2.20 pm; here we visited the signal box in the hazy sunshine before the return departure at 3.00 pm, the five loaded sugar beet wagons being left there. John and Brian rode in the cab of the 03.

On the return trip wagons of sugar beet were collected at Skipwith along with some empty vans. At Dunnington the locomotive carried out extensive shunting before adding two wagons of sugar beet, two covered vans and a grain silo wagon on its way to Scotland. Arrival at Layerthorpe was at 5.22 pm.'

Part of the tonnages carried around this period consisted of large quantities of sugar beet. In 1964 the harvest was so bountiful that special trains were arranged with BR to transport the beet to the refinery at Nottingham, two of these trains being run each week during the harvest season, each of 500 tons. Similarly bumper potato crops in 1965 and 1966 led to considerable quantities needing to be transported to Goole docks, ironically these could

have been easily transported via the then recently closed Cliff Common, and Selby lines to their destination.

As has been seen during the 1960s and 1970s further sections of the line were closed until, by the end of 1972, it only ran between Layerthorpe and Dunnington. An article in the *Railway Observer* at this time reported that the usual weekly traffic was between 12 and 24 grain wagons to Dunnington, 10 bogie oil wagons to Layerthorpe yard, 'Presflo' wagons for Osbaldwick and beet traffic from Dunnington, although 1972 was be the last year for the latter. Roger Darsley reported that around this time there were an average of 24 bulk grain vehicles handled each week, along with cement wagons each day. In addition, there were two oil trains for the Layerthorpe depot per week in winter, plus a shunt each day at the coal plant.

By Autumn 1974 the shorter line length meant that the daily train had been moved to the afternoon, and this was the situation on 2 October 1974 when a trip along the line was reported on. This report stated that the train departed Layerthorpe with DVR No.1 hauling nine bulk grain wagons, a load of about 107 tons, at 1.45 pm. The loco crew had to keep a sharp watch on the line as there had been numerous incidents of vandalism with objects being placed on the track.

At Osbaldwick they collected two cement wagons, making the load 130 tons, and proceeded towards Murton passing the construction site for the new York by-pass en-route. Meanwhile at the site of Murton station the scrapyard was busy, and there were plans for a rail-served depot to

Above: It was not unknown for wagons to be propelled as well as pulled along the line, as seen here in this photo of one of the company's diesel shunters on the line at Metcalfe, or Osbaldwick, Lane crossing on 17 November 1972.   (Photo: R.R. Darsley)

bring in materials for the by-pass. Going on towards Dunnington the train passed Dunnington sewerage works, before reaching Dunnington itself. Here the grain driers' shunting locomotive, *Churchill*, took charge of the grain wagons, before No.1 and the two cement wagons returned to Layerthorpe, the whole trip having taken one and three-quarter hours.

In the latter years of the 1970s the line was improved. This was to allow axle loadings to increase so that larger grain wagons could be run. Meanwhile the yard at Layerthorpe could now take 100 ton bogie tank wagons, which were stored there when not in use during the summer. However, come the late 1970s and early 1980s traffic dropped dramatically, which led to the decision to close the line.

Left: DVR No.1 *Lord Wenlock* passes the remains of Murton Lane station on 17 July 1979 with a train of bulk grain wagons.

(Photo: R. Patrick)

Layerthorpe

Above: Class J21 No.65064 at Layerthorpe station having arrived back with the Branch Line Society special on 17 May 1958. It had run non-stop from Cliff Common, supposedly the first passenger working to do so.

(Photo: D.A. Kelso Copyright Colour-Rail BRE1541)

When the DVLR was built the station at Layerthorpe lay on the eastern edge of the city of York. There was a marsh to the south and Tang Hall beck flowed along the southern edge of the site. This made the station subject to flooding, which was so severe in 1947 that the service locomotive had to be kept at Osbaldwick. The station was constructed beside the NER's Foss Islands branch with road access from Hallfield road.

Layerthorpe was the headquarters of the line and had the most extensive layout of any of the stations. The station building and the general manager's office were, like the other stations on the line, what were known as 'Composite Buildings' as outlined in an article in *The Locomotive* in March 1915.

These buildings were made up from sheets of compressed asbestos and cement mounted in a timber frame. This, the article claimed, not only had cost and durability advantages, but could also produce attractive buildings. Similar buildings had previously been used on the Grassington branch constructed by the Yorkshire Dales Railway Company, for whom Edgar Ferguson had been the engineer. On the DVLR the building frames were painted green, while the panels were a cream colour. In 1968 the station buildings between Layerthorpe and Elvington were repainted in light grey and stone, although they do

appear to have been repainted with green framing later.

A 528 ft radius curve connected the DVLR's main line to the NER's Foss Islands branch. There was also a gate which could be closed across the tracks to delineate the boundary between the companies. Goods trains could run directly through Layerthorpe station by-passing the platform. This was because the platform, on the north side of the main line, could only be accessed directly from the Cliff Common direction. Locomotives were released through a trailing connection onto the main line. In addition there was another run-round loop on the south side of the main line.

The station platform itself was 300 ft long and 22 ft wide at its widest point, and still on a sharp curve. On the south side of the southern run-round loop there was another siding. Meanwhile on the north east side of the station was a goods yard. This had four sidings accessed from a headshunt at the Cliff Common end. In the yard there was a large series of cattle pens and a goods shed, as well

Above: In the DVLR archives there is a series of what appears to be 'official' photographs of their buildings taken c. 1923. This is the main station building at Layerthorpe with possibly the stationmaster standing on the left.

Right: The general manager's office at Layerthorpe, the nameplate now proclaiming the occupant to be Mr W.T. Grundy although he is not in the photograph.

(Both Photos: DVLRS/YMF Archive)

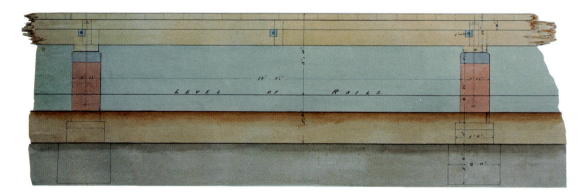

Above: Original drawing showing the detail of the wooden station platform construction, which was supported on brick piles. It is worth comparing this with one of the actual platforms in the top photograph. The drawing is reproduced at approximately 7mm to the foot.

Left: From the same set of photographs comes this view of the goods warehouse at Layerthorpe.

Right: Originally there was a large series of cattle pens at Layerthorpe, but these were reduced as time passed. It appears that by this time electric lights had been installed in the yard. Two of the DVLR's coaches can be seen in the background.

(Both Photos: DVLRS/YMF Archive)

Below: The interior of the ticket office at Layerthorpe reproduced to approximately 7mm to the foot.

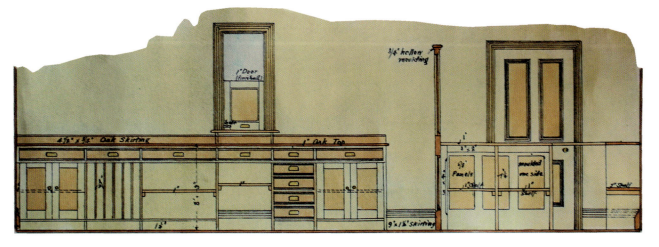

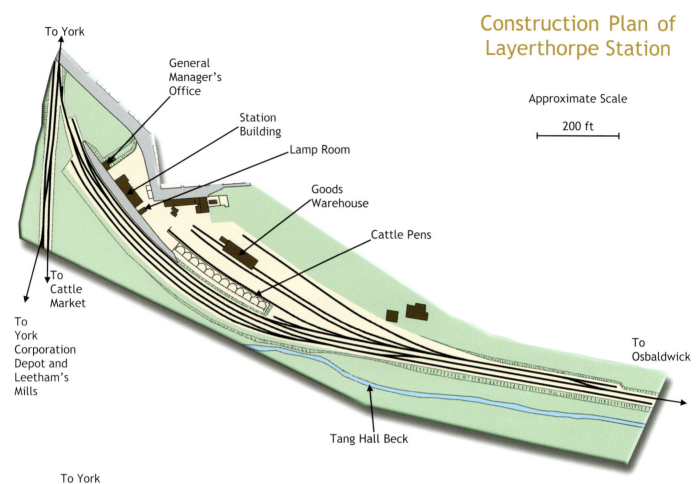

Construction Plan of Layerthorpe Station

To York

General Manager's Office

Station Building

Lamp Room

Goods Warehouse

Cattle Pens

Approximate Scale

200 ft

To Cattle Market

To York Corporation Depot and Leetham's Mills

Tang Hall Beck

To Osbaldwick

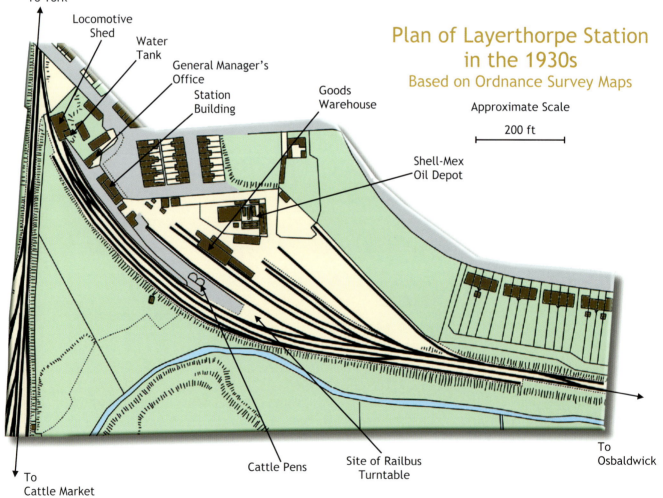

Plan of Layerthorpe Station in the 1930s
Based on Ordnance Survey Maps

To York

Locomotive Shed

Water Tank

General Manager's Office

Station Building

Goods Warehouse

Shell-Mex Oil Depot

Approximate Scale

200 ft

To Cattle Market

Cattle Pens

Site of Railbus Turntable

To Osbaldwick

Above: This view of Layerthorpe yard featured on the front cover of the *Derwent Farmers' News* for January 1936. A fine range of private owner coal wagons can be seen on their 'standings' in the yard, while on the left is LNER class N12 No.2485 originally built for the Hull and Barnsley Railway. Also in the picture is Mr S.J. Reading, the general manager at this time, standing second from the left behind the locomotive. (Photographer Unknown DVRCo Archive)

as a weighbridge.

In 1915 'Asiatic Petroleum', a joint venture between Shell and the Royal Dutch Oil Company, opened a terminal on the northern edge of the goods yard. This seems to have been taken over in 1919 by Shell themselves (known as Shell-Mex Ltd from 1921), and it was probably around this time that a fifth siding was added to the yard.

Coal merchants also rented 'standings' on the sidings. Here coal wagons could be based with supplies for distribution around the city. Other occupants of the yard at this period were a small tarmacadam plant, a depot for india rubber waste, and a yard for the storage of water pipes. Fertilisers were also stored in the Company's warehouse. A sixth and seventh siding were laid in the late 1920s/early 1930s when the yard was also extended to the north.

Another change at Layerthorpe, which occurred in 1924, was the construction of the turntable at the end of a spur road near the cattle pens to turn the railbuses on. No engine shed was provided before this time, as the NER's locomotive and crew would return to their home shed at the end of each duty. However, when the DVLR started to provide their own crews the locomotives could be stabled on the line overnight, and in the late 1920s a wooden locomotive shed was constructed on the headshunt at the north west end of the station platform.

There were other improvements such as the provision of electric lighting, and piped water laid to the cattle pens. In addition, all the fencing at the back of the station platform was made demountable so that loads could be removed from trains at the platform easily.

In World War Two the yard was used for the storage of coal both by the local coal merchants, and also by the York Corporation Electricity Department. It also became a railhead for aviation fuel to supply some of the local aerodromes. After the war new coal pens were built from concrete blocks, and also garages provided for the coal merchants' lorries constructed from 'Nissen' huts, with further garages added in the 1950s.

Then in the early 1960s a large coal distribution plant was built in the yard, which was opened on 12th October 1964 with its own dedicated siding. In 1966 43,000 tons of coal and coke were delivered to the plant, with two trains arriving there daily during times of peak demand.

As mentioned earlier on 15 July 1967 there was a serious fire in the engine shed, which also damaged a diesel shunter stood inside. The locomotive shed was subsequently rebuilt to house the DVLR's own locomotives.

During the early 1970s the main line and sidings at Layerthorpe were relaid with concrete sleepers, as well as heavier rail to permit the running of 100 ton oil

Aerial View of Layerthorpe Station in May 1939

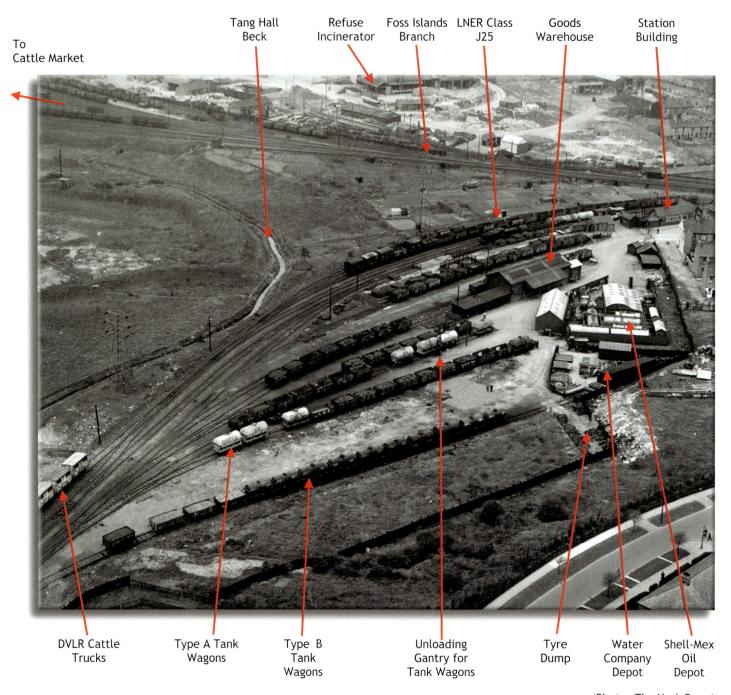

To Cattle Market — Tang Hall Beck — Refuse Incinerator — Foss Islands Branch — LNER Class J25 — Goods Warehouse — Station Building

DVLR Cattle Trucks — Type A Tank Wagons — Type B Tank Wagons — Unloading Gantry for Tank Wagons — Tyre Dump — Water Company Depot — Shell-Mex Oil Depot

(Photo: *The York Press*)

tankers. The layout was also changed with the south side run-round loop being truncated to a siding, while in the yard the number of sidings was reduced to three, the one serving the coal plant having its own run-round loop. Later in 1977 two further sidings were removed.

In the 1960s the station buildings were reconstructed with modern office space being provided. When the line was opened the original staff compliment at Layerthorpe was one stationmaster, Mr J.W. Steel, and no less than four porters. This was gradually reduced over the years particularly with the demise of the passenger service.

The coal plant closed in August 1980, and with the end of services to Dunnington in September 1981, the only traffic on the DVR was the oil tankers. These only needed to access the former station area, where the oil depot was re-equipped to handle them. In addition a number of them were stored in the sidings opposite the old platform during the slack months between July and December. This continued until October 1988, the movements being done by BR locomotives after the closure of the main line, when Layerthorpe finally closed. Today the station has all but been obliterated, and the site is now occupied by the Ebor industrial estate and a DIY superstore.

Above: There was a repeated problem with flooding at Layerthorpe as this view from 1937 shows. Even after the war the area continued to flood, despite numerous efforts to remedy the situation. Sheila Robson, the daughter of the last general manager, Jim Acklam, remembers how they used to lasso floating sleepers to prevent them drifting away.

(Photographer Unknown DVRCo Archive)

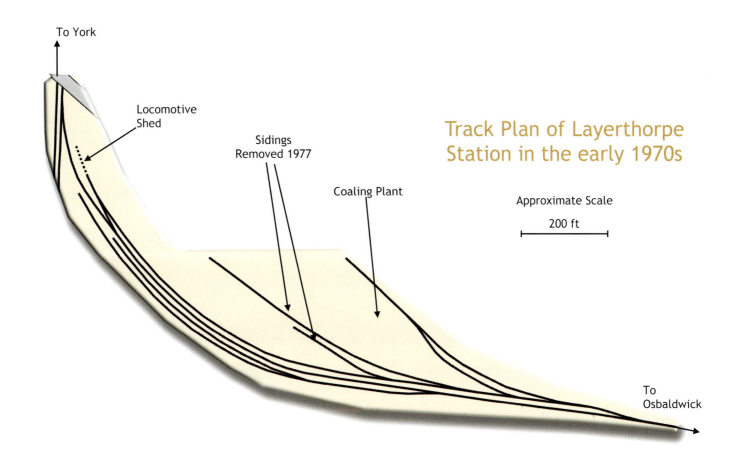

To York

Locomotive
Shed

Sidings
Removed 1977

Coaling Plant

Track Plan of Layerthorpe Station in the early 1970s

Approximate Scale

200 ft

To
Osbaldwick

Above: BR class J25 0-6-0 No.65714 at Layerthorpe shed on 4 August 1959 during the visit of members of the Wakefield Model Railway Society.
(Photo: R. Redman)

Right: The doors of Layerthorpe shed stand open in September 1960. The water tower was erected shortly after the line opened, but the shed itself did not appear until around 1928. This was, ironically, just before the railway sold its only locomotive.
(Photo: N. Coulthard)

Left: Driver's eye view of Layerthorpe yard from the footplate of J25 No.65687 on 9 May 1953. On the right can be seen some tank wagons beside the unloading gantries. York Minister can also be glimpsed in the left background.
(Photo: C.H.A. Townley
Copyright Industrial
Railway Society)

Above: A larger than usual visitor to Layerthorpe yard was ex-War Department 2-8-0 No.90518, which had been purchased by BR in 1948. It was there on 21 July 1964 with an engineering train working on lifting sidings on the Foss Islands branch.
(Photo: David J. Mitchell)

Above: On the same day as the photo above, BR class 03 D2112 shunts in Layerthorpe yard while on the right the coal distribution plant is under construction.
(Photo: David J. Mitchell)

Left: Another visitor to Layerthorpe yard in the shape of a class 20 No.8018, which passes DVR No.2 on the right on 25 February 1970.

(Photo: J.H. Meredith)

Right: *Joem* at Layerthorpe with the train for Dunnington on Friday 31 August 1979. This was the final day of the regular steam service.

(Photo: J.D. Stockwell)

Left: *Joem* departs for Dunnington in 1979.   (Photo: P. Rounce)

Left: The old general manager's office can be seen amidst the jumble of buildings at the northwest corner of the station site, with the rebuilt loco shed in the background on 18 May 1977.
(Photo: David J. Mitchell)

Right: After the official closure of the line *Churchill* was brought up to Layerthorpe in preparation for sale. It is seen here outside the re-built loco shed on 11 October 1981.
(Photo: P. Rounce)

Below: Layerthorpe station building continued to be used as the offices for Appletons oil depot, and the road side of the building is seen here in 1982. (Photo: J.D. Stockwell)

Osbaldwick

Above: Ex-LMS Ivatt No.46409 heads the joint RCTS/SLS North Eastern Tour down the line, and is about to pass under Tang Hall Lane bridge on 27 September 1963. (Photo: David J. Mitchell)

From Layerthorpe the line ran eastwards on the level across a small embankment. On the south side there was a tarmacadam plant during the war, which was served by its own siding complete with run-round loop. Now on a slight gradient of 1 in 660, and curving gently towards the north east the track passed over Tang Hall beck. This was the only substantial underbridge on the line. Beyond this, just before Melrosegate or Tang Hall bridge, there was another wartime installation on the south side of the line. This was an ordnance depot that handled Ford engines and spares, which was served by two sidings off the main line.

The line now passed under the bridge. It was erected in the late 1920s, as the north and south side of the line beyond this point started to be developed, with the railway contributing towards the costs. At the same time Tang Hall beck was culverted, and the underbridge was removed.

Left: Load restriction notice on Tang Hall Lane bridge.
(Photo: J.D. Stockwell Collection)

Still climbing, the line now passed through a cutting. This was the scene of constant problems through the years with stones being thrown at the trains and objects placed on the track. The people of the area also used the railway as a shortcut, and the children a play area. Driver Raymond Howden recalled a particularly close call involving two young children on the track, where a fatality was only narrowly avoided. Frequent letters and articles were published in the local paper speaking of the issues and the dangers. The problem was that, after the end of passenger services, there was generally only one train a day in each direction, giving the impression that the line was near derelict.

After this the first of the two original overbridges was reached at Tang Hall Lane, just over half a mile from Layerthorpe. This, until post-World War Two, represented the boundary of the York conurbation, with the land beyond becoming increasingly rural.

Once the bridge was passed the grade stiffened to 1 in 150 and the next landmark was Osbaldwick, or Metcalfe, Lane crossing, just over a mile and a quarter from Layerthorpe. On the north side of the line just before the crossing an electricity sub-station was built in the early 1930s. This was served by its own siding off of the main line.

The siding was unusual in that it passed under the sub-

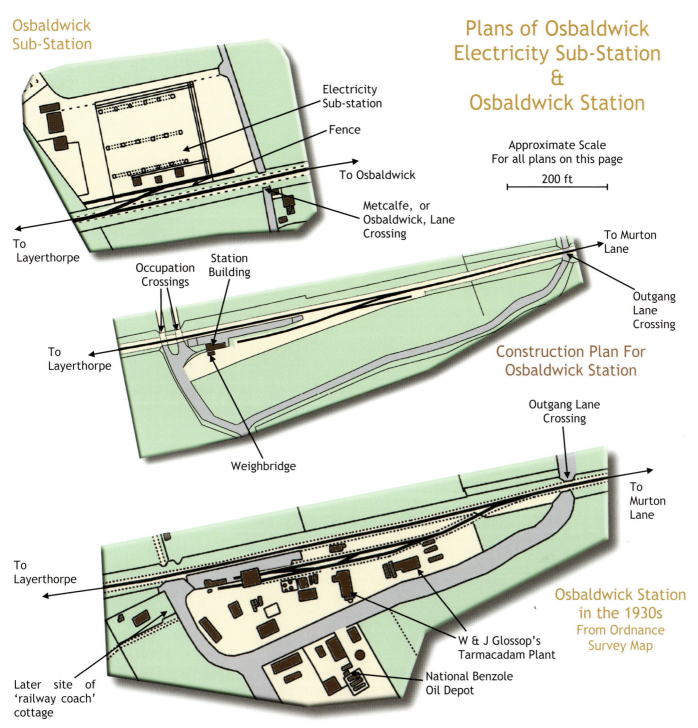

Osbaldwick
Sub-Station

Plans of Osbaldwick
Electricity Sub-Station
&
Osbaldwick Station

Electricity
Sub-station

Fence

To Osbaldwick

Approximate Scale
For all plans on this page

200 ft

Metcalfe, or
Osbaldwick, Lane
Crossing

To
Layerthorpe

Occupation
Crossings

Station
Building

To Murton
Lane

Outgang
Lane
Crossing

To
Layerthorpe

Construction Plan For
Osbaldwick Station

Weighbridge

Outgang Lane
Crossing

To
Murton
Lane

To
Layerthorpe

Osbaldwick Station
in the 1930s
From Ordnance
Survey Map

W & J Glossop's
Tarmacadam Plant

Later site of
'railway coach'
cottage

National Benzole
Oil Depot

station fence rather than through a gate, the fence having to be removed when the siding was required. It was to this sub-station that a transformer, the largest load ever transported on the DVLR, was conveyed in 1931. In 1932 the railway transported 3,000 tons of materials to the site. The sub-station siding lasted in service until 1968 when the whole installation was dismantled.

In the 1970s this crossing also became the source of a major dispute with the local farmers when, following a Ministry of Transport inspection, crossing gates were re-erected. After much debate consideration was given to making the crossing open with flashing lights, but, as the complaining parties were unwilling to contribute to the cost, the alterations were never made.

From the crossing the line levelled, and there was a

platform on the south side of the line. This was built for York Corporation for the unloading of cattle. At just under a mile and three-quarters from Layerthorpe the line came to two adjacent occupation crossings, before Osbaldwick station was reached.

The original intention was to have a loop here, but, before the line was opened, a new station was added to the plans at Murton Lane, and the loop laid there. Meanwhile Osbaldwick was reduced to the status of a halt. It had a single 200 ft long platform and station building on the south side of the line, along with a single siding and headshunt. Originally it was manned by a solitary porter, but it was a short-lived passenger station, disappearing from the timetables by autumn 1915.

However, in the 1920s, W & J Glossop, a firm of tar

Left: In June 1922 the DVLR altered the yard at Osbaldwick as part of the construction of Glossop's tarmacadam plant (Below). This included the provision of a run-round loop in the yard, the crossover for which is being finished off in the photo to the left. The DVLR's travelling crane has also been employed on this work.

(Photo: L. Bradley Courtesy R.A. Whitehead)

Left: Osbaldwick station in 1935, with some tank wagons at the National Benzole unloading gantries.

(Photo: Ronald Shephard Courtesy West Sussex Record Office)

distillers famous for their fleet of Sentinel steam lorries, moved into the station yard and constructed a tar distillery. This resulted in the original siding being extended and a second one added in 1922, with a crossover to allow locomotives to run-round, while the headshunt was removed. Glossop's remained at the station for many years.

National Benzole also had a depot here, established in 1927, on the other side of Outgang Lane on the south side of the station. Oil was unloaded from the wagons in the yard and piped into the storage tanks. Their tank wagons were often seen in the daily pick-up trains before the war and after.

Unlike other stations Osbaldwick did not see major developments during the war, but in the 1950s, like many other sites up and down the line, the site was used for the storage of timber. Then in 1959 a ready-mixed concrete firm, Site Supply and Excavation Co Ltd, set up shop in the station yard. As a result in 1965 'Presflo' 20 ton cement wagons became a staple traffic for the railway travelling between Layerthorpe and Osbaldwick.

There was now only one siding at the station, but in 1965 a replacement siding was laid to handle full length trains of the 'Presflo' wagons. Today there is still a ready-mix cement plant at Osbaldwick, while the rest of the station site is now occupied by a builders' merchants.

One other interesting structure at Osbaldwick was just over the road from the station. Here there was a cottage constructed from two old coaches. Its occupant for many years was Rubins Metcalfe, who was employed as a platelayer on the line from 1941. His letter of employment stating that a requirement for the job was to be able to ride a bike. This was so that he could get to the other end of the line quickly if required. The cottage lasted until January 1993 when it was demolished, the origins of the coaches are unknown, but from the photographs they do not appear to be the former coaches used on the DVLR.

Left: Osbaldwick station looking towards Layerthorpe as seen on 27 April 1954. Part of a Glossops lorry can be seen on the left, and a tar lorry in the background.
(Photo: J.J. Davies Copyright Historical Model Railway Society)

Right: Ex-NER and LNER class J25 No.65677 shunts at Osbaldwick on 4 January 1955.
(Photo: Peter T. Hay)

Left: The house constructed from two carriages that was home to DVLR platelayer Rubins Metcalfe for many years.
(Photo: E. Hearfield)

Right: On 21 July 1964 D2112 arrives at Osbaldwick station with the daily pick-up goods.
(Photo: David J. Mitchell)

Left: Shunting at Osbaldwick in 1963.   (Photo: R. Holdsworth)

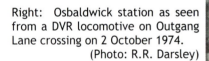

Right: Osbaldwick station as seen from a DVR locomotive on Outgang Lane crossing on 2 October 1974.
(Photo: R.R. Darsley)

Left: The site of Osbaldwick station as seen from Outgang Lane crossing in April 2013. A travellers' site now occupies most of the north side of the trackbed, and has spilt out onto the trackbed itself, on the left is the builders' merchant while the cement plant is in the background.
(Photo: I. Drummond)

Left: The previously mentioned Directors' Special on 25 September 1981 having passed over Osbaldwick Road crossing. It is now on the course of the revived Derwent Railway Light Railway.
(Photo: Stephen Chapman)

Right: The initial stages of making the bridge for the York by-pass over the line, as seen from the footplate of one of the DVR shunters, looking towards Murton Lane on 2 October 1974. (Photo: R.R. Darsley)

Left: Further along the line the locomotive approaches Murton Lane crossing and the station beyond. The setting still looking quite rural at this time. The train is actually at the site of Murton Park station on the revived DVLR today. (Photo: R.R. Darsley)

Murton Lane

Above: Slightly backwards geographically *Joem* passes over Osbaldwick Road crossing before passing under the York by-pass in 1977. This is now the end of the revived DVLR today. (Photo: Stephen Chapman)

From Osbaldwick the line continued on the level over a gated crossing across Outgang Lane. After this the line turned east again over Osbaldwick Beck, and after a quarter of a mile came to the gated Osbaldwick crossing. This crossed the Osbaldwick and Murton Road, now known as Murton Way. Here a pair of cottages was provided, one for the crossing keeper, and the other for a permanent way ganger. Today the eastern side of the crossing is the western terminus of the revived Derwent Valley Light Railway.

Now the line is climbing on a grade of 1 in 660, just before the modern bridge built in the mid-1970s that carries the A64 York by-pass across the line. During the construction of the road a temporary occupation crossing was made here for the contractors. However, some cavalier driving on the part of the latter led to some near misses with approaching trains.

At this point the line is running more or less due east and it levels out before reaching Murton Lane. Today the terminus of the revived railway is on the western side of the lane, but originally the line crossed the lane into Murton Lane station just over two and a half miles from Layerthorpe. This station was not in the original plans, but was added in 1911. The 200 ft long station platform was on the south side of the line, immediately adjacent to the gated crossing.

Beyond the platform there was a loop line, from which a siding was laid to the south of the station platform serving a cattle pen and horse dock. Looking at the 1930s Ordnance Survey plan (see opposite) the loop appears to have been built shorter than the original construction plan. In addition to the main station building a tariff shed, lamp hut and weighbridge were provided. The station staff on opening consisted of a stationmaster and porter, the stationmaster being Mr W. Wilkinson, who also had oversight of Osbaldwick.

In 1927 Russian Oil Products (R.O.P.) established a depot here, for distribution of their R.O.P. petrol. During World War Two the site was requisitioned to become the Northern Command Petrol Depot. Trains transported petrol and oil to the site where it was stored in cans in the station yard, and over the adjoining fields. At its peak there was an estimated 500,000 gallons stored in and around the station.

For this traffic the layout at Murton was changed with an additional siding laid capable of holding forty wagons. By 1949 the loop line had been removed and there were two

D.V.L.R. SECOND CLASS.
YORK (Layerthorpe)
TO
MURTON LANE
Fare 6d.
0553
See Back.

extended sidings in the station yard. There was also an additional trailing siding on the north side of the line.

After the war in 1947 a private-owner wagon repair and dismantling yard was established in the station yard. By the 1970s this had become a scrapyard, served by a siding. The loop was also re-established at some point, formed from the north side trailing siding. It is reported that during a steel shortage fifteen wagon loads of scrap were being transported each week from the yard.

When the by-pass was being built in the 1970s some of the construction materials seem to have been brought in here as well. Today the scrapyard occupies the site, and nothing of the original station remains.

Plans of Murton Lane Station

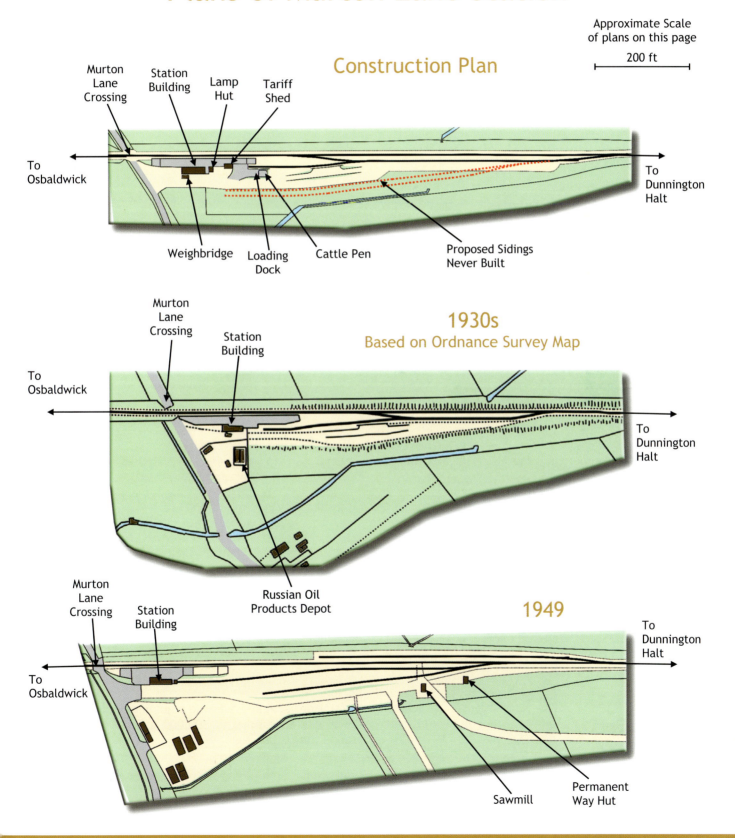

Approximate Scale of plans on this page

200 ft

Construction Plan

Murton Lane Crossing
Station Building
Lamp Hut
Tariff Shed

To Osbaldwick

To Dunnington Halt

Weighbridge
Loading Dock
Cattle Pen
Proposed Sidings Never Built

1930s
Based on Ordnance Survey Map

Murton Lane Crossing
Station Building

To Osbaldwick

To Dunnington Halt

Russian Oil Products Depot

1949

Murton Lane Crossing
Station Building

To Osbaldwick

To Dunnington Halt

Sawmill
Permanent Way Hut

Original drawing of the halt buildings for Osbaldwick, Murton Lane, Dunnington Halt and Cottingwith reproduced at approximately 3mm to the foot. (Murton Lane and Osbaldwick were the mirror image of this drawing).

Left: Class J25 No.65714 shunting at Murton Lane on 4 August 1959.
(Photo: R. Redman)

Right: Shunting tank wagons, probably for scrapping, at Murton Lane on 7 June 1960.
(Photo: V. Nutton Courtesy Travel Lens Photographic)

Left: On 9 January 1965 the penultimate special to Cliff Common passes through Murton Lane station. At some point an extension with a second gable was added to the station building.
(Photo: David J. Mitchell)

Right: The last train through Murton on 27 September 1981. (Photo: P. Rounce)

Left: Just six months after closure this was the scene with the track lifted and the scrapyard spilling over the trackbed.
(Photo: David J. Mitchell)

Above: On the north east side of Sledmere, or Stamford Bridge Road, crossing there was a siding installed in 1928, originally for both sugar beet and minerals. After the beet trade ended the siding was still used for storage, and was still in use in 1974. Ex-BR class 04 DVR No.1 is photographed shunting wagons for sugar beet in the siding on 30 October 1969.   (Photo: J.H. Meredith)

Above: On 27 September 1981 the last train traverses Sledmere crossing on its return to Layerthorpe.   (Photo: P. Rounce)

Dunnington Halt

Above: The 'official' company photograph of Dunnington Halt c. 1923, consisting of a single platform and building situated by Dunnington bridge.
(Photo: DVRS/YMF Archive)

Beyond Murton Lane the rural nature of the line resumed. It climbed on a grade of 1 in 264, which stiffened to 1 in 150 just east of the station. The line then carried on due east through the fields, until the gated Sledmere crossing was reached three miles from Layerthorpe. Here two cottages were provided on the south east side of the crossing. Just beyond the crossing a wooden loading platform was built in 1928. This was served by a trailing siding allowing for sugar beet and minerals to be loaded. After the beet trade finished it was used for storage, the pigeon brake being among a group of vehicles noted there in 1974.

After Sledmere crossing the line entered the major earthwork on the line, Dunnington cutting, which was some 21 ft deep at its deepest point and extended for over half a mile. By this time the line had climbed to the highest point on the route, 67 ft above sea level, before levelling and then falling at 1 in 150. It now passed under the last overbridge on the railway. This carried Dunnington Lane over the line, and immediately after the bridge Dunnington Halt was reached three and a half miles from Layerthorpe.

Here there was a single 200 ft long platform provided on the north side of the line. It had a station building that was the mirror image of those at Osbaldwick and Murton

Lane. This was the closest station to Dunnington village, although it was still a reasonable walk from the village itself. There were no sidings or any other facilities provided.

The main function of the halt was for passengers, and so when the passenger service ceased, it had little purpose. However, the station building continued to be used and in 1947 a newspaper article reported on the Tindall family. They then occupied the station building, and the article commented on the fact that their drinking water was delivered each day by train. In fact a similar arrangement applied at several of the railway's properties, which were not connected to the water mains.

Excursions did not usually stop at Dunnington Halt, but on 16 January 1965 an RCTS organised railtour, in connection with the closure of the line from Wheldrake to Cliff Common, did stop there. This became the last recorded passenger train at the station. By the late 1960s the station had been demolished, and there were only the overgrown remains of the platform by the time the line closed in 1981.

Left: Again the official photograph of Dunnington bridge taken c. 1923. (Photo: DVLRS/YMF Archive)

Below: On 4 August 1959 Ron Redman got this view from the cab roof of No.65714 with its train at Dunningon Halt. (Photo: R. Redman)

Left: There was obviously a chance for a 'photo opportunity' at the halt that day with the loco and crew being photographed from various angles.

(Photo: R. Redman)

Left: On 21 July 1964 BR class 03 D2112 passes with the daily goods train, which no longer called at the station. The station building is clearly still occupied at this time, with the platform becoming more of a garden!
(Photo: David J. Mitchell)

Right: By the time of the penultimate passenger train to call at the station, on 9 January 1965, it appears that the 'garden' has been cleared. This was possibly a sign the building is now unoccupied, certainly it seems to have been demolished not long after.
(Photo: David J. Mitchell)

Left: By 1981, when DVR No.1 *Lord Wenlock* passes the site on 16 September, there is little left. Neighbouring gardens having been extended onto the site, and nature has done the rest.   (Photo: David J. Mitchell)

Dunnington (for Kexby)

Above: No.46409 continues its journey south to Cliff Common on 27 September 1963 reaching Dunnington with the RCTS/SLS railtour.
(Photo: David J. Mitchell)

After leaving Dunnington Halt the line was now on a bend which took the line south east on a small embankment. It was still falling at 1 in 150 for a further half a mile past the sewerage works, until it levelled and then entered Dunnington station. The station was situated at Four Lane Ends, four and a quarter miles from Layerthorpe. It was on the crossroads of what was to become the A1079 between York and Hull, and Common Road.

In fact the station was known as Dunnington (for Kexby), and often simply Kexby, even though Dunnington was nearly a mile away and Kexby more or less two. Therefore it served neither community satisfactorily. It is not surprising then that, when the passenger service was operating, it was not the busiest station in the world. For example, the station records stated that for the week ending 9 October 1920 nine singles and one return to Layerthorpe were sold on Monday plus one 'blank' single; one single and a return to Layerthorpe, as well as three 'blank' singles on Tuesday; three singles to Layerthorpe, two 'blank' singles and a contract (or season) on Wednesday; five singles to Layerthorpe on Thursday; two singles to Layerthorpe on Friday; and on the Saturday eight singles and seven returns to Layerthorpe, one contract and a dog!

The track layout at Dunnington changed little over the years until the late 1970s. As a train entered from Layerthorpe there was a loop line to the east of the main line, from this two sidings were laid. One was a long one, which in later years served the grain driers, and there was also a shorter spur road. This initially served a loading dock and cattle pens, before the latter were removed. After passing through the trailing point for the loop, trains would then arrive at the station. Once more there was a 200 ft long platform with a station building, and the train would come to rest with the locomotive nearly at the crossing over the Hull Road.

In 1917 a timber yard was established at the station. Then, after the end of passenger services, the station building was leased to Norman W. Dunn & Co Ltd. They were a firm of road contractors, who were to remain at the station for many years. Dunn's also appear to have extended the station building.

There were also advertising hoardings at the station, taking advantage of its position next to the main road. These promoted a variety of products and services, including Butlins holiday camps.

Left: An early postcard of Dunnington station building showing it in its original form.
(Commercial Postcard)

Right: The stationmaster's house at Dunnington now part of a day nursery.
(Photo: DVLRS/YMF Archive)

During the war there was relatively little development at Dunnington. This seems slightly surprising considering that it also had easy road access. Possibly it was to allow it to continue to be a major centre for agricultural produce, particularly sugar beet. One change that did occur was that the original 6 ton weighbridge was replaced with a 20 ton one.

However, after the conflict there were some changes, new coal pens were built in concrete, and the station was used for the storage of timber during the 1950s. J.L. Fridlington and Co Ltd also built a potato warehouse at the station in the late 1940s, complete with a carrot washing station. There was even a hand-worked narrow gauge railway to move goods around for loading or unloading from their store.

The original staff at the station on opening was a stationmaster and two porters. Mr W.J. Privett, was the first stationmaster, who also oversaw Dunnington Halt and lived in the house provided on the site. With the end of passenger services the need for staff was reduced. However, in 1947 it is recorded that there were two members of staff. Mr R.A. Todd was the porter-in-charge

along with a porter, Mr R. Andrew. This probably reflected the amount of agricultural produce being handled there.

In 1955 a major new industry came to Dunnington in the form of Yorkshire Grain Driers Ltd, which was to provide a steady flow of traffic almost up until the closure of the line. The first grain was shipped out in 1956, and was destined for Distillers Co Ltd at Bathgate in Scotland. As the plant developed the level of automation increased, with bulk grain hoppers being used from 1958. Eventually the firm procured their own locomotive, a Fowler 0-4-0 diesel shunter named *Churchill*. This arrived in 1971 and was used to shunt the grain hoppers slowly past the filling station, as well as for other duties.

As mentioned in the history in the mid-1960s a parcel of ten acres of land was purchased, which the DVLR began to develop as an industrial estate in the 1970s. From 1972 Dunnington was the terminal station on the railway, and as such was also the end of the line for the steam trips in the late 1970s. As a result there are numerous photos of *Joem* by the level crossing gates, which had been replaced in 1956, from that time. In addition the long siding was shortened, and the siding to the loading dock lifted.

After the end of the steam passenger services the main line down to the platform was removed. The layout now consisting of two dead-end sidings to allow further land to be developed. *Churchill* was used to release the train

locomotive of incoming goods trains.

The remaining track was taken out of use with the rest of the line in September 1981, and was soon lifted. Today the Derwent Valley Industrial Estate has obliterated the station with very little remaining, save for the stationmaster's house which forms part of a day nursery.

Plans of Dunnington Station

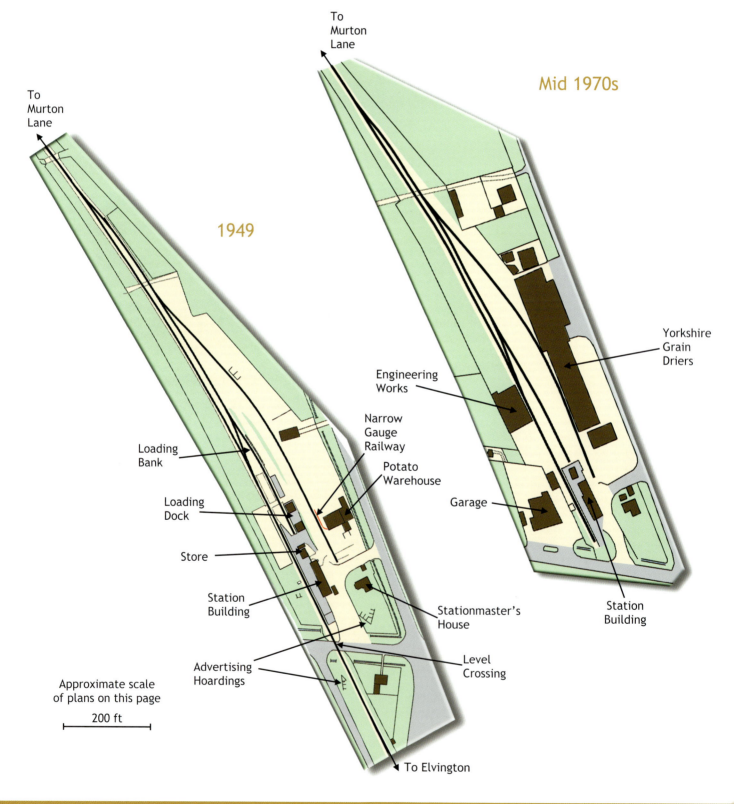

To Murton Lane

Mid 1970s

To Murton Lane

1949

Yorkshire Grain Driers

Engineering Works

Narrow Gauge Railway

Loading Bank

Potato Warehouse

Loading Dock

Garage

Store

Station Building

Station Building

Stationmaster's House

Advertising Hoardings

Level Crossing

Approximate scale of plans on this page

200 ft

To Elvington

Right: The road side of Dunnington station building. This was also the offices for Norman W. Dunn road contractors, who had extended the building at the far end and on the platform side. In addition the weighbridge can be seen just to the right of the nearest corner of the building.
On 7 April 1956 the daily goods train, with a single coach for an excursion party, stands at the platform en-route to Cliff Common.
(Photo: J.C. Halliday)

Below: On 9 May 1953 class J25 No.65687 stands at the platform with the daily goods train for Cliff Common. There was an oil depot based in the goods yard, and a couple of tank wagons can be seen in the right background. In addition a couple of 'Nissen' huts had been built since the 1949 survey.
(Photo: C.H.A. Townley Copyright Industrial Railway Society)

Right: Dunnington station on 27 April 1954 showing the platform side extensions to the building. Obviously a train was not expected imminently judging by the Imperial College student standing in the middle of the tracks!
(Photo: J.J. Davies Copyright Historical Model Railway Society)

Right: With its position by the main road between York and Hull the DVLR made the most of the location by erecting advertising hoardings, such as this one on the south side of the crossing. Certainly the advert for 'Cobnut' sliced tobacco, which proclaims that 'it is good' rings slightly hollow today. (Photo: J.C. Halliday)

Below: On 21 July 1964 D2112 and the daily goods had made it to Dunnington where some shunting was carried out. (Photo: David J. Mitchell)

Right: The last-but-one passenger train to Cliff Common pauses at Dunnington on 9 January 1965. A loading 'hump' had been created in the platform in front of the loco by this time. (Photo: David J. Mitchell)

Right: DVR No.1 with an impressive train of covered wagons at Dunnington on 27 May 1972. Behind the locomotive is the grain driers building, while in the background behind the last wagon is the station building.

Below: A more general view of the station yard during the same shunt. *Churchill* can be glimpsed with some bulk grain wagons in front of the grain driers building on the left.
(Both Photos: David J. Mitchell)

Right: *Joem* stands at the buffer stops at Dunnington on 18 May 1977 after arriving with the steam service from Layerthorpe. Notice that the station building had been repainted by this time.

(Photo: David J. Mitchell)

Left: The site of Dunnington station platform and building in April 2013 taken from the far side of the former crossing. By this time the only DVLR building is the former stationmaster's house, which can be seen on the extreme right.

Right: Soon after the end of the steam service the track into Dunnington station was lifted, and the line cut back to release more land for development. A sign of things to come.
(Photo: David J. Mitchell)

Left: The last days of the DVR on 16 September 1981 as *Churchill* shunts grain wagons, and tank wagons are unloaded at Dunnington. DVR No.1 *Lord Wenlock* waits in the distance.
(Photo: David J. Mitchell)

Right: Ken Bell, the DVR's last driver, climbs aboard *Lord Wenlock* in preparation for taking the train back to Layerthorpe.
(Photo: David J. Mitchell)

Left: Class J25 No. 65677 starts the daily goods away from Dunnington on 4 January 1955 heading towards Elvington. The train contained a significant number of cattle trucks on that day. To the left of the rearmost vehicle is the advertising hoarding, by the road. The stationmaster's house can be glimpsed over the open wagons.
(Photo: Peter T. Hay)

Right: No.46409 departs from Dunnington on 27 September 1963, the track is almost obliterated by the weeds at this point.

(Photo: David J. Mitchell)

Left: On 21 July 1964, D2112 can be seen on the same section of line with a somewhat shorter train. It was even shorter than previously as the open wagon has been left at Dunnington during the previously observed shunt.
(Photo: David J. Mitchell)

Elvington (for Sutton)

Above: BR class J25 No.65714 shunting at Elvington c.1957. There is evidently a party of enthusiasts travelling with the train as at least two of them are getting a ride on the loco. (Photo: David A. Lawrence Copyright Colour-Rail 309061)

Once the train had crossed over the Hull Road it now headed south east across what was once Dunnington Common. It climbed for quarter of a mile at 1 in 220, before the line levelled for another quarter of a mile passing over an occupation crossing. There was then another crossing serving White Carr House. After this the line then fell in various stages for a mile and a half, passing beside Dodsworth woods and through part of the Escrick estate. Then, after passing over another occupation crossing, about half a mile short of Elvington (for Sutton) station, the line curved to be running more or less due south into the station six and a half miles from Layerthorpe.

The early layout at Elvington seems to have been similar to that at Dunnington. Trains passing through a loop which had a long siding leading off it, along with a short spur road to a loading dock, before entering the station platform. This was adjacent to the level crossing over the B1228, which ran to Elvington originally some half a mile from the station.

At first the station had a stationmaster, Mr H.J. Silke, and two porters. Mr Silke lived in one of two

cottages provided, while the other cottage was home to one of the gangers. The porters lodged in the village. For most of its life the stationmasters there, later known as porters-in-charge, came from one family, the Handleys, with no less than three generations holding the position.

Elvington station's relative remoteness from both Elvington and Sutton upon Derwent, led to an experimental bus service being laid on in June 1914. This was run by a Mr A. Dawson, on behalf of the DVLR, to bring passengers from the villages to the station on Mondays, Tuesdays, Thursdays and Saturdays. However, it seems to have had little success.

There was though one steady form of traffic, anglers. They made use of the station on Saturday afternoons on their way to the Derwent, and special tickets were issued for them. One observer commented that he saw about twenty making their way to the river on one occasion.

After the passenger service ceased Elvington continued to be a major centre for the farmers in the area. As a result it was one of the first stations to have a telephone installed in 1927, with the number Elvington 11. By this the stationmaster could be contacted to make arrangements for the delivery and pick-up of goods, hiring of wagons etc. The station was also one of the centres for the railway's delivery and collection service.

Left and Below Left: Scenes as the opening train arrived at Elvington on 19 July 1913. The local vicar had organised the welcome party, and the train remained at the station for fifteen minutes during its journey to Cliff Common. Mr Silke, the stationmaster, can be seen on the left of the bottom photo.
(Photos: Hanstock Postcards)

Below: Handbill for the bus service provided for the villagers of Elvington and Sutton Upon Derwent in 1914.

DERWENT VALLEY LIGHT RAILWAY.

PASSENGER AND PARCELS 'BUS

To and from Elvington Station,

COMMENCING SATURDAY, JUNE 13th, 1914.

Sir or Madam,

For the convenience of the public, arrangements have been made with Mr. A. Dawson, of the "Grey Horse Inn," Elvington, to run a 'Bus for the conveyance of Passengers between the villages of Sutton and Elvington, and Elvington Station, in connection with the following trains :—

Monday, 10- 7 a.m., to Cliff Common.	Thursday, 8-22 a.m., to York.
4-25 p.m., from "	" 11-35 a.m., "
Tuesday, 11-35 a.m., to York.	" 1-24 p.m., from York.
" 5-39 p.m., from "	" 5-39 p.m., " "
Saturday, ALL TRAINS.	

Passengers will be conveyed FREE by 'Bus to and from the Station on condition that they purchase from the Carrying Agent a return railway ticket to York or Cliff Common, or any other D.V. Station to which the return fare is 1s. or over for adults and 6d. or over for children under 12 years of age.

Passengers taking return tickets at any other D.V. Station to Elvington Station, with a fare of not less than 1s. adults and 6d. children, will be given a 'Bus ticket on arrival at Elvington by the above trains, entitling them to travel free in the 'Bus to either village.

Other passengers not complying with above conditions may use the 'Bus by making their own fare terms with the Carrying Agent.

There will be no increase in railway fares either on Market or Ordinary Days, but for the present the "Free" arrangement only applies to the trains named above, and subject to the 'Bus accommodation being sufficient. If after a start has been made the 'Bus is found to be inadequate, a larger vehicle will at once be put on.

However, it was during the Second World War that Elvington station took on a major role with materials being brought in for the construction of Elvington aerodrome a mile west of the station. The air station became operational in October 1942, after which Elvington station saw many shipments of ammunition and ordnance delivered to supply the bombers. All this activity led to a new siding being laid to the west of the main line, capable of holding twenty wagons.

After the war Thomas W. Ward Ltd opened a wagon repair and dismantling business in the station yard. A new storage warehouse was also constructed. Then, in 1965, there was a major development when the DVLR purchased a parcel of land on the north east side of the station. This was then leased to Agriform Fertiliser Ltd. They built a plant for the production of liquid fertiliser there, which opened on 11 October 1966. There were hopes of additional rail traffic being generated, and an extra siding was laid with loading facilities for tank wagons. However,

in the end the Company decided to go with road transportation for the bulk of its trade.

On 14 May 1968 the last train ran from Wheldrake to Elvington with the line being abandoned shortly after. This left Elvington as the terminus of the line and dependent on the agricultural traffic. However, when it was known that the sugar beet traffic was coming to an end, the decision was taken to truncate the line back to Dunnington. It is said that the last train ran from Elvington on 22 June 1972, but the line was not officially abandoned until the December.

Although the railway sold the trackbed between Elvington and Dunnington they retained the station yard, but they did sell it at a later date. Today the fertiliser plant is still operational having been expanded and is now owned by Yara UK. There is little left of the station itself, save for the former railway cottages.

Above: The cottages provided by the railway at Elvington.
(Photo: DVLRS/YMF Archive)

Plan of Elvington Station in 1949

Approximate Scale

200 ft

Below: The six and a half milepost at Elvington.
(Photo: J.J. Davies Copyright Historical Model Railway Society)

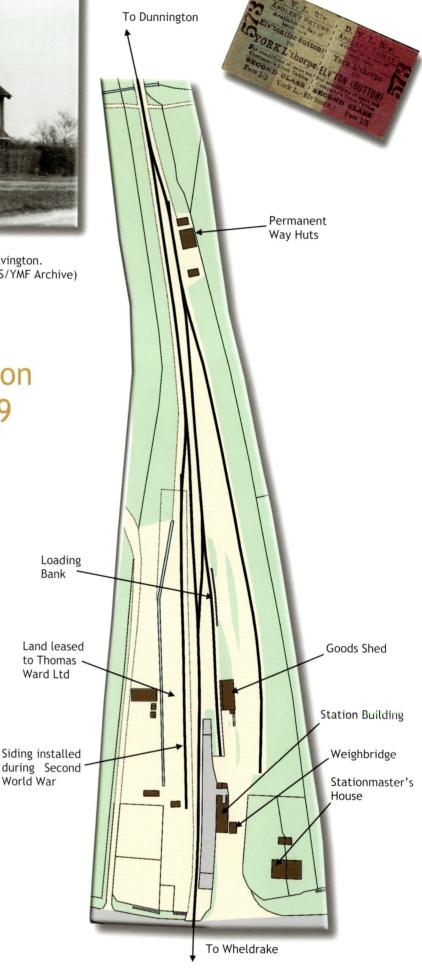

To Dunnington

Permanent Way Huts

Loading Bank

Land leased to Thomas Ward Ltd

Goods Shed

Station Building

Weighbridge

Siding installed during Second World War

Stationmaster's House

To Wheldrake

Left: LNER Class N12 No.2486 at Elvington with a goods train in the 1930s.
(Photo:J.K. Perkin Copyright J.B. Perkin)

Right: On a decidedly damp and misty day in September 1960, class J25 No.65714 is shunting at Elvington. The cab sheet is firmly pulled over to keep the worst of the weather out.
(Photo: N. Coulthard)

Left: Class J25 No.65700 stands at Elvington station on 8 September 1952.
(Photo: W.S. Garth Copyright Photo Archive Stephenson)

Left: A view of Elvington station buildings through the cab window of No.65714 in September 1960.
(Photo: N. Coulthard)

Right: The point lever and Annett locking mechanism at the north end of the station.
(Photo: J.J. Davies Copyright Historical Model Railway Society)

Right: Elvington station buildings with members of the Imperial College Railway Society on 27 April 1954.
(Photo: J.J. Davies Copyright Historical Model Railway Society)

Left: An interesting view of Elvington yard while shunting takes place. Note the piles of stored timber stacked on the right.
(Photo: W.S. Garth Copyright Rail Archive Stephenson)

Above: A general view of Elvington station taken on 27 April 1954 looking south east towards Wheldrake.
(Photo: J.J. Davies Copyright Historical Model Railway Society)

Above: In the siding on the left a line of condemned wagons await scrapping. Meanwhile J25 No. 65677 shunts in the station on 4 January 1955. The sign on the right makes interesting reading as it advertises 'King-Fish Manures' from the Crown Manure Co Ltd of Hull. These products were stored in the goods warehouse. It also looks like part of the station building roof is being renewed.
(Photo: Peter T. Hay)

Above: D2112 heads through Elvington with the return working from Wheldrake and Cliff Common in the early 1960s.
(Photo: Copyright Transport Treasury)

Right: Members of the Wakefield Railfans Club enjoy some fun with a platelayers' trolley at Elvington during their trip down the line on 22 November 1961. Peter Smith is on the left with Brian Moss on the right.
(Photo: J.W. Holroyd)

Left: On 21 July 1964 the daily goods train hauled by D2112 arrives at Elvington from Dunnington.
(Photo: David J. Mitchell)

Left: In October 1966 the Agriform fertiliser plant opened, which is seen here on the right in this photo from 1967, also note the piles of sugar beet awaiting collection by the trackside.
(Photo: Ronald Shephard DVRCo Archive)

Right: The last regular working to Wheldrake departs on 14 May 1968 with guard Arthur Todd leaning out of the cab of class 03 D2054. Two tankers can just be seen in the Agriform plant siding in the background.
(Photo: R. Wildsmith)

Left: The end of the line. Elvington had been the terminus of the DVLR after the line to Wheldrake closed in 1968. However, in 1972 the line between Dunnington and Elvington also closed, although the Company retained the land at Elvington station for potential industrial development. It is seen here on 27 May 1972 shortly before the last train ran on 22 June 1972.
(Photo: David J. Mitchell)

Left: Away from the stations some locations, such as the crossing at the former Elvington Brickyard, were rarely photographed, but David Mitchell helpfully got two photographs there. The first shows the 1963 tour at the crossing with No.46409 on 27 September, with the crossing keeper's house just visible on the right. There was a loop line here, which had at least one siding off in the area on the right of the photo. Due to the grass and weeds it is hard to tell whether the rails are still in-situ.
(Photo: David J. Mitchell)

Right: The RCTS special of 9 January 1965 passes the loop before the crossing on its return run from Cliff Common. The wagon in the loop probably belonged to the DVLR. By this point any additional sidings had definitely been removed.
(Photo: David J. Mitchell)

Left: Another of these rarely photographed location was the next crossing at Broad Highway. However, D2054 on the last working to Wheldrake is seen here on 14 May 1968. The siding for the sugar beet traffic installed in 1927 was on the right of the crossing on the far side of the track.
(Photo: R. Wildsmith)

Wheldrake

Above: No.46409 rounds the curve through the cutting, past the nine milepost, on the approach to Wheldrake on 27 September 1963. The famous Wheldrake signal, the only one on the line, can be glimpsed in the background. (Photo: David J. Mitchell)

After the level crossing at Elvington the line started to curve south west and climb for half a mile on a gradient of 1 in 660. It then levelled out for a quarter of a mile before reaching the site of Elvington Brickyard. At this point the line crossed the road between Elvington and Wheldrake over a gated crossing, with a crossing keeper's lodge on the south east side.

The brickyard seems to have been operational from the mid-nineteenth century, and presumably was one of the those referred to by Lord Wenlock at the public inquiry. In October 1913 the DVLR applied for permission to lay a loop at the site, although there is no record of an inspection of the facility. One certainly did exist,though, in the 1950s and 1960s. Plans also indicated that there was at least one further siding in the 1950s. However, brick making at the site seems to have ended in the 1930s.

Still running south west for three-quarters of a mile the line then came to Broad Highway crossing. Here, in later years the crossing was ungated, but the 'official' photo of the crossing keeper's lodge taken in the 1920s shows gates in place. A siding and platform for loading sugar beet was built on the north east side of the crossing in September 1927, capable of holding nine or ten wagons.

During the war it is recorded that bombs were unloaded here for Elvington aerodrome. After this the line ran for another half a mile before encountering the most

commented on feature of the journey, the single signal at Wheldrake.

One of the ideas before the line was built was to have the road bridge over the line at Wheldrake. Later this was revised with the line climbing at 1 in 264 through a shallow cutting on a curve. It was then heading due south where it crossed the road, which had been lowered so that the two could intersect on the level.

The upshot of this was that approaching the crossing from Elvington the train driver was 'blind' to the state of the gates. Therefore, after the line opened, a signal was constructed at the Sand Hutton estate, home of the famous Sand Hutton Railway, a few miles away. It was connected to the crossing gates so that the signal was 'off' when the gates were open to rail traffic, and set at danger when the gates were closed. Construction of the signal itself consisted of a wooden post with a fishtail arm, which was painted red in the manner of the early distant signals.

Having traversed the crossing over the road, the line now entered Wheldrake station situated on the western edge of the village, nine

Left: The 'official' photo of Wheldrake station c. 1923. Note the construction of the platform which can be clearly seen in this photograph, meanwhile the stationmaster's house can be glimpsed on the right.
(Photo: DVLRS/YMF Archive)

pumped through them. Burner-jets were positioned at intervals to produce walls of flame which had the effect of dispersing the fog. This meant that aircraft could be diverted to Melbourne from other fog-bound aerodromes. Similar systems were installed at fifteen other aerodromes.

Some 1,921,680 gallons of petrol was handled at Wheldrake in just under two years, two tanker trains arriving each week when required. One day an extra train arrived, but there was no storage available, so the jets were lit and 50,000 gallons of fuel burnt in a single sunny day. However, despite its extravagant use of fuel, it is estimated that 'Operation FIDO' saved something like 11,000 lives.

miles from Layerthorpe. On the east side of the line, adjacent to the crossing, was the now familiar 200 ft long platform and station building. Beyond this there was a loop with long and short sidings off, the latter serving a loading dock and cattle pen.

However, it is clear from the construction plans that Wheldrake was intended to be the major intermediate station on the line. There was provision for an extended goods yard with two further sidings, and even a full length loop running from the crossing to the southern station limit. In the event none of these materialised, It did, though, have the only locomotive water supply on the line between York and Cliff Common in the shape of a 2,000 gallon 'parachute' tank supplied from a well.

Initially the staff allocation was one stationmaster, Mr R. Gilbank, who lived in the house on site and no less than three porters. This again indicated the significance the railway thought the station would have. It was, after all, the one intermediate station on the line that was actually convenient for the village it served. But clearly the reality did not match up, because by 1947 the station had lost its stationmaster, and there was now a porter-in-charge Mr F. Stabler, while Eric Howden later occupied the post.

As stated previously, during the Second World War Wheldrake station yard was taken over by the Royal Engineers for unloading bombs. These were stored in the yard, as well as on the verges of the local roads. This must have been slightly unnerving for anyone driving in the locality, especially in the dark. Wheldrake was also used for petrol trains supplying Operation FIDO, which was based at Melbourne aerodrome.

FIDO or the 'Fog Investigation and Dispersal Operation' was developed at Birmingham University. It consisted of pipelines laid along both sides of the runway with fuel

Following the war there were further developments, a range of eight 'Nissen' huts were erected for the storage of fertiliser, while in the 1950s the lineside was used for the storage of timber. In 1952 the Ministry of Works purchased part of the southern end of the station site to create a 'buffer' store. This was mainly used for the storage and supply of sugar, as well as other foodstuffs such as corned beef, flour and biscuits in case of nuclear war. Thousands of tons of goods were received and sent out by rail while it was in use.

The next major development at the station occurred in January 1965 when the line to Cliff Common was closed, and Wheldrake became the southern terminus of the line. However, with the decline in traffic as the various depots either closed, or switched to road transportation, soon the section to Wheldrake was only really carrying sugar beet traffic.

Therefore, it was decided to close the line from Wheldrake to Elvington. On 14 May 1968 the last train ran from Wheldrake, which consisted of two 'Presflo' wagons and the ex-LNER pigeon brake. Thus Wheldrake would seemingly pass into history.

But this was not quite the end, at least not for the station building, for just over thirty years later it found itself once more serving passengers. This was because it had been dismantled and reassembled at the Yorkshire Museum of Farming to serve the revived Derwent Valley Light Railway.

Plans of Wheldrake Station

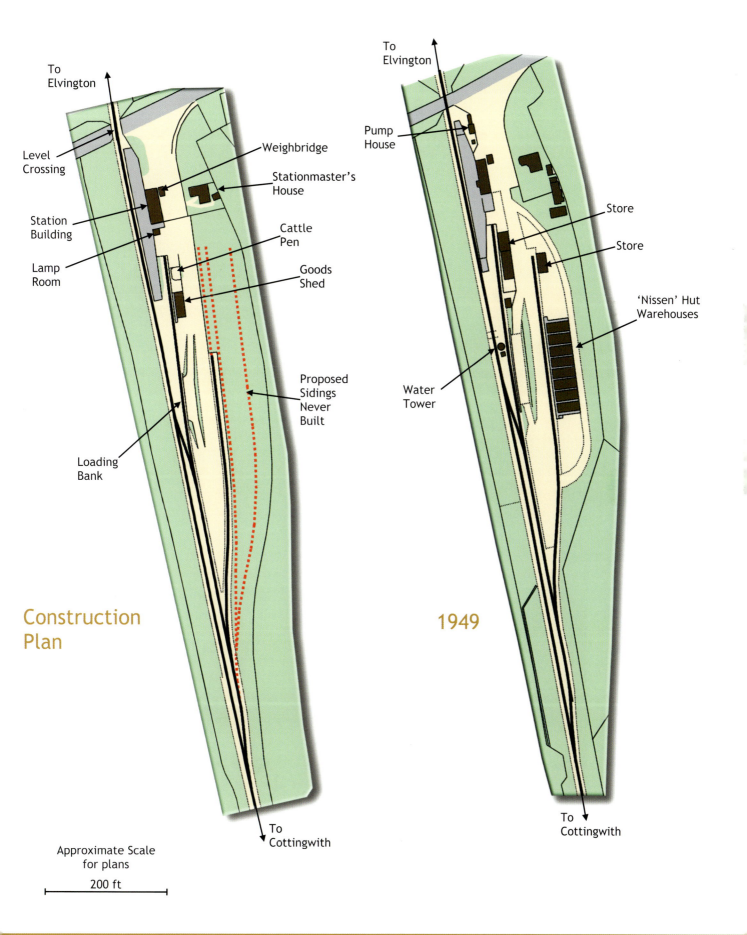

To Elvington

Level Crossing

Station Building

Lamp Room

Weighbridge

Stationmaster's House

Cattle Pen

Goods Shed

Loading Bank

Proposed Sidings Never Built

To Cottingwith

Construction Plan

To Elvington

Pump House

Store

Store

'Nissen' Hut Warehouses

Water Tower

To Cottingwith

1949

Approximate Scale for plans

200 ft

Right: The water tower at Wheldrake. Although this was not on the original construction plan it was in place by opening day. Evidently life at the stations could be informal, as witnessed by the goat and chicken wandering the yard on the left.
(Photo: DVLRS/YMF Archive)

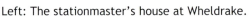

Left: The stationmaster's house at Wheldrake.
(Photo: DVLRS/YMF Archive)

Below: A general view of Wheldrake station looking south in the mid 1950s. In the far background the newly constructed 'buffer' store (No.543/E) can be seen. On the platform there are some sacks, and what appears to be a stack of sawn up sleepers, awaiting collection. The notice to the left of the crossing tells visitors that if the buffer store is closed they should phone Selby 340. Attached to the lower hinge on the nearer gate is the chain which operated the signal in the cutting. (Photo: W.S. Garth Copyright Rail Archive Stephenson)

Above: Possibly the most photographed signal in Britain was the one warning drivers of the state of Wheldrake crossing. John Holroyd captured this picture of it on 22 November 1961.   (Photo: J.W. Holroyd)

Above: The fireman takes a break as the tanks on class N12 No.2486 are filled from the water tower in the 1930s.
(Photo: J.K. Perkin
Copyright J.B. Perkin)

Right: The hut where the pump to draw water from a well for the station, including the water tower, was housed.
(Photo: Ken Nelson)

Left: No.65677 at Wheldrake on 4 January 1955 prepares to depart for Cottingwith. The corner of the buffer store can be seen on the right.
(Photo: Peter T. Hay)

Right: The view from the cab as No.65714 approaches Wheldrake on 27 June 1957.
(Photo: B. Connell Copyright Photos From The Fifties)

Left: No. 65700 takes water at Wheldrake on 8 September 1952.
(Photo: W.S. Garth Copyright Rail Archive Stephenson)

Left: D2112 and train arrives at Wheldrake on 21 July 1964.
(Photo: David J. Mitchell)

Right: Shunting at Wheldrake by the buffer store building on 21 July 1964.

(Photo: David J. Mitchell)

Left: The last train from Wheldrake on 14 May 1968, driven by William Watson.
(Photo: R. Wildsmith)

Left: The remains of Wheldrake station in 1982. Fortunately the station building was later dismantled for re-erection at the revived Derwent Valley Light Railway at the Yorkshire Museum of Farming, Murton Park.
(All photos this page J.D. Stockwell)

Right: The decaying remains of the 'Nissen' huts at Wheldrake in 1984, the three huts at the far end appear to have collapsed completely.

Left: The former goods shed in 1984. It has had some end doors added since the line closed.

Cottingwith

Above: D2111 and the RCTS Special reaches Cottingwith on 9 January 1965. The boundary fence for the Forward Filling Depot (FFD5) is still in place, and the remains of the siding can also just be glimpsed in the long grass.   (Photo: David J. Mitchell)

From Wheldrake the line ran more or less due south descending on gradients of 1 in 264, 1 in 165 and 1 in 220 for three-quarters of a mile. It then ran level for the next half mile before approaching Moor Lane crossing and Cottingwith station ten and a quarter miles from Layerthorpe.

Moor Lane crossing was the only crossing over a public road that was originally ungated. On the original plans there was simply going to be a halt just south of the crossing, named Moor Lane Halt. This would have been on the same lines as Dunnington Halt, with a 200 ft wooden platform and halt building.

However, with construction under way in January 1912 this was changed. A loop was put in on the north side of the crossing and a loading dock. There was even a siding pencilled in, construction of which was still being considered in 1914. Meanwhile the halt remained on the south side of the crossing with the platform on the east side of the line, but the name was changed to West Cottingwith station.

In the event the station opened as simply Cottingwith. It has to be said though, that the opportunities for passenger traffic were very limited. It was a good mile by road from West Cottingwith, and East Cottingwith could only be reached by ferry across the Derwent. Therefore, it is probable that the end of passenger services did not have a huge effect at Cottingwith, with the station building being converted to a house at a cost of £18 15s.

Cottingwith was also the location of the previously mentioned fatal crash on 11 August 1937, when Mrs Edith and Miss Elizabeth Cape were killed following a collision between their car and the daily goods train. As a result of this additional signage was erected at the crossing.

As is evident the main reason for the station was for agricultural traffic, which was the station's staple for most of its life. The exception to this occurred during the Second World War, and into the 1950s, when the Escrick Forward Filling Depot (or FFD5 as it was known) was built to the north west of the crossing.

This was for the storage of mustard gas, and also for preparing weapons for use in combat during World War Two, despite chemical weapons having been banned under

Construction Plan for Cottingwith Station

Plan of Forward Filling Depot Five and Cottingwith Station
From Ordnance Survey Map

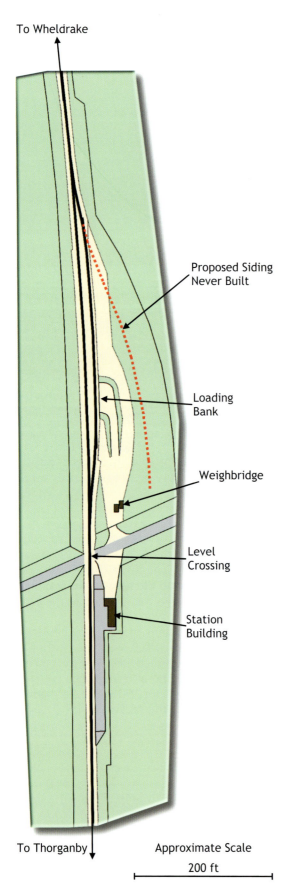

To Wheldrake

Proposed Siding Never Built

Loading Bank

Weighbridge

Level Crossing

Station Building

To Thorganby

Approximate Scale
200 ft

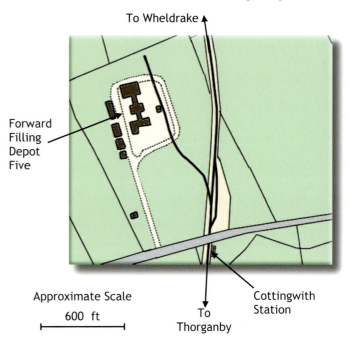

To Wheldrake

Forward Filling Depot Five

Cottingwith Station

To Thorganby

Approximate Scale
600 ft

the Geneva Protocols. The gas was produced at ICI's Randle plant near Runcorn and transported to the Escrick facility, which was one of five forward filling depots in use by 1944, by train.

Facilities at FFD5 consisted of storage sheds for empty weapon cases, a bonding shed and a charging shed where the bombs were loaded. There were also two underground storage tanks where the gas was stored in a liquified form, the depot being capable of holding up to 500 tons. In addition there were changing and decontamination rooms, as well as mess facilities. To bring materials in and out of the site a siding was laid from the loop at Cottingwith to the bonding shed (see plan above).

Weapon charging at the site finished at the conclusion of the war. Through the early 1950s the gas was removed from the site; the last being transported away by train in 1954, before being disposed of at sea. Ken Nelson remembers a mustard gas train going through Skipwith to Cliff Common. Luckily his mother had the 'box Brownie to hand', and although she cannot remember the precise date, she thinks it dates to the early 1950s.

But the area was not fully decontaminated until the 1990s. Even then there was a large cache of ammunition found buried in a field in 2011 which was probably associated with the depot.

With the closure of the depot the station was overwhelmingly dependent on the agricultural traffic. By 1961 the station building had been demolished with only the platform remaining until the line closed in 1965. Today all traces of the railway and halt have gone with the land returning to agricultural use, save for the remains of FFD5 which still exist there.

Left: Cottingwith station building was the mirror image of the buildings at Osbaldwick and Murton Lane. After the end of passenger services it was converted into a house. (Photo: DVLRS/YMF Archive)

Right: On 4 January 1955 No.65677 shunts at Cottingwith. The siding to the depot can be seen descending on the grade to the left. This was the only piece of track south of Dunnington to have ever been laid with concrete sleepers.

Below: Locomotive No.65677 has now crossed the road and is seen in front of the old station.

(Both Photos: Peter T. Hay)

Left: The railway's revenge; as one of the trucks of Marple and Gillott, who were responsible for lifting the line south of Wheldrake, gets stuck in the mud at Cottingwith in February 1966.
(Photo: David J. Mitchell)

Right: The remains of FFD5 on 8 April 2011.
(Photo: J.D. Stockwell)

Above and Right: What appears to be an Ivatt class 4 2-6-0 passes through Skipwith station in the early 1950s, photographed from outside the stationmaster's house. However, the train was carrying a sensitive load to say the least, in the form of tanks of mustard gas, loaded into open wagons. We are fortunate to have these glimpses of what was essentially a 'clandestine' operation.
(Photos: Lavinia Nelson)

Thorganby

Above: No.46409 approaches Thorganby on 27 September 1963.

(Photo: Copyright Ernie Brack)

After Cottingwith the line continued south climbing for just under quarter of a mile at 1 in 350 then for a further half a mile at 1 in 660. During the latter part of the climb the line passed over South Moor Lane crossing, just under half a mile from Cottingwith. This was gated with a crossing keeper's lodge provided. It was the site of a proposed station that would have originally served both Cottingwith and Thorganby. Having reached the top of the ascent, the line then ran level for a quarter of mile, before climbing again to Thorganby Road crossing on a grade of 1 in 660. It then entered Thorganby station just under eleven and a half miles from Layerthorpe.

The opening layout consisted of the usual 200 ft long platform and station building with a loop line beyond, only this time with just a single spur line serving a loading dock and cattle pen. There was provision made within the plans for two more sidings to be laid. However, in the event the layout remained the same throughout the life of the station.

Indeed Thorganby seems to have been the least changed station on the line. Even the war brought little new activity, save for the ongoing loading and unloading of agricultural produce and supplies. This is testified by the following memory from a local farmer Norman Patrick. He used to live with his father at Horn Farm, just north of the station at Thorganby in 1939 and recalled those days along with the role of the railway:

"Farm work included many trips to our local railway station (Thorganby), as we grew potatoes, sugar beet and cereals almost everything we needed and used seemed to come in trucks. Potato sets would come from Scotland carefully wrapped round with straw ... in a covered wagon... for us to collect.

Sugar beet lifting began in October ...This was hard work .. as the beet was pulled and topped with a knife or spade, thrown into heaps ... and taken to the railway station. Most farmers liked a good big wagon to get beet quickly to Selby beet factory. It was important for farmers to keep on good terms with the local stationmaster ...in war-time wagons were sometimes hard to find.

Before threshing days could be organised railway sacks must be ordered well in advance from the railway station ... it was all railway sacks loaded into covered wagons.

I well remember my Dad buying Irish store cattle at York market, and they would turn up at Thorganby station in cattle trucks.

Then my Dad, my brother and I would drive them home about a quarter of a mile down the railway to Horn Farm."

After the war the station settled back into its quiet routine, unchanged except for the building of some new coal pens, and the provision of a 'Nissen' hut as a store around 1950. The station closed with the line between Wheldrake and Cliff Common in 1965.

Left: 'Official' photograph of Thorganby station c. 1923.
(Photo: DVLRS/YMF Archive)

Right: Early postcard of Thorganby station from the main road.
(Commercial Postcard)

Left: The stationmaster's house at Thorganby.
(Photo: DVLRS/YMF Archive)

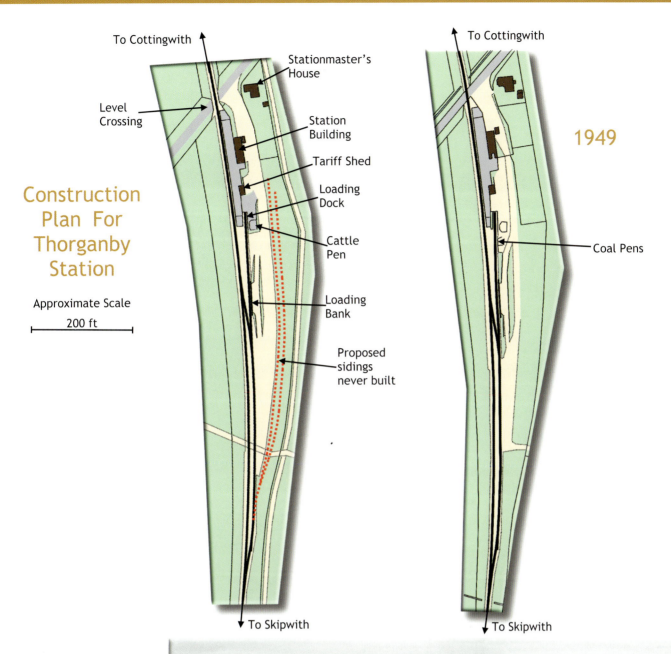

Construction Plan For Thorganby Station

Approximate Scale

200 ft

To Cottingwith

Stationmaster's House

Level Crossing

Station Building

Tariff Shed

Loading Dock

Cattle Pen

Loading Bank

Proposed sidings never built

To Skipwith

1949

To Cottingwith

Coal Pens

To Skipwith

Right: Class J25 No.65700 pauses at Thorganby. The class J25s had no vacuum braking, as signified by the lack of a vacuum pipe on the bufferbeam, and so were used for goods traffic with loose coupled wagons. (Photo: W.S. Garth Copyright Rail Archive Stephenson)

Right: D2111 enters Thorganby station with the last but one up excursion on 9 January 1965.
(Photo: David J. Mitchell)

Left: The remains of Thorganby station in 1985.
(Photo: J.D. Stockwell)

Right: Thorganby station building in April 2013, permission is being sought to allow the building's restoration.
(Photo: I. Drummond)

Skipwith (and North Duffield)

Above: Some onlookers await No.46409 passing Skipwith having nearly reached the end of its journey down the line.
(Photo: David J. Mitchell)

From Thorganby the line now turned south west, gently undulating for nearly a mile and three-quarters. In 1911 thought was given to building a branch line westwards at this point to Manor Farm, which is just off the Skipwith to Escrick road, but in the end no further moves took place. Skipwith station was now reached, some thirteen miles from Layerthorpe and the last intermediate station.

At Skipwith station itself the original plans were for the station to be laid out south of the road crossing in the same manner as Wheldrake and Thorganby. However, a dispute with the landowner led to new plans being drawn up for the station to be built north of the crossing, the land eventually being acquired late in 1911 for £500. Initially the station had a similar layout to Thorganby with a loop on the York side of the platform, along with a short spur line serving a loading dock and cattle pen. However, Skipwith began to take on a more significant role as it became the terminus for most of the passenger services from York.

In the mid-1920s a new siding was laid off the loop using track that had been lifted from Cliff Common. In addition, a turntable was installed opposite the station platform and a 50 ft long running shed built for the railbuses. These were accessed by a trailing siding from the main line.

As far as convenience for passengers was concerned it was the same old story, with the station being half a mile from the village. This was reflected in the traffic receipts with only two or three pounds worth of tickets being sold each week, most of these being on a Monday or Saturday. After the end of the regular passenger services, the station was used as the terminus for the 'Blackberry Specials' which ran in the 1920s and 1930s, as noted earlier. Porter-in-charge at Skipwith, Henry Howden and his wife Mabel, acted as guides taking people off over Skipwith Common.

The Howdens had been at the station almost since the line opened, and ended up remaining there for 43 years. Ken Nelson, Henry's grandson, and his mother, Lavinia Nelson, have given an interesting insight into life at Skipwith, which will be dealt with in more detail later. After Henry's retirement his son, Eric became porter-in-charge until that section of the line closed. In addition one of the original permanent way gangs, which was based at Skipwith, were responsible for the line between Wheldrake and Cliff Common. They had their own hut in the station yard.

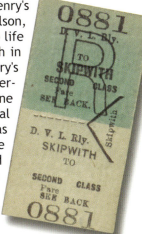

Agricultural produce and coal were

the main traffic at the station, both before, and after, World War Two. The sugar beet harvest could be a particularly busy time. Even a horse was hired to help with the shunting, the lack of an Annett key to operate the ground frame being overcome by unscrewing the cover plate and operating the points manually!

Once a day the pick-up goods would come through Skipwith. As it passed over the occupation crossing north of the station the train locomotive would give a coded whistle to indicate whether it had traffic for the station or not. Thursday was cattle day, and in the evening the cattle pen could be overflowing, with cattle in the station yard waiting to be driven to the farms. There was also some parcel traffic. This included day old chicks, with Henry Howden needing to phone the farmers to tell them to come and pick them up.

During the war Skipwith was used as a staging point for materials used in the construction of Riccall aerodrome.

Ken Nelson remembers an asphalt plant being constructed at the station for the aerodrome work, and also the unloading of the bombs for the base. He also recalls the American GIs, some of whom were black, something of a culture shock in rural East Yorkshire at the time.

Just after the war a new set of coal pens was constructed, and around 1950 three 'Nissen' hut structures were built. One was on the platform, with another behind the loading dock. Meanwhile the third smaller hut was at the northern end of the station, possibly for permanent way stores. In 1958 another larger warehouse was built in the station yard.

Today the station is home to passenger carriages once again. The site has been converted into a self-catering holiday base, using ex-main line Mark Two coaches as high class accommodation. In addition the station building has been tastefully restored as a private residence, retaining many of the original features.

Plans of Skipwith Station

Construction Plan

To Thorganby

Proposed Siding

Cattle Pen

Tariff Shed

Station Building

Weighbridge

Loading Bank

Loading Dock

To Cliff Common

Approximate scale for plans

200 ft

1949

To Thorganby

Permanent Way Hut

Siding laid c. 1924

Grounded brake van body

Stationmaster's House

Coal Pens

Remains of Railbus turntable

To Cliff Common

Left: An interesting photograph of the railbuses at Skipwith in 1924 apparently on a trial run. To the right of the photograph building work appears to be going on, probably for the turntable and running shed for the railbuses.
(Photo: Ken Nelson Collection)

Right: Skipwith station probably just post-war before the 'Nissen' huts were added on the platform, and behind the loading dock.
(Photographer Unknown DVRCo Archive)

Left: On 4 January 1955 No.65677 pauses at Skipwith while some goods are loaded from the platform. The stationmaster's house can be seen in the background.
(Photo: Peter T. Hay)

Left: A view across the yard at Skipwith in the early 1950s. Note the loading gauge, the only one known on the DVLR, probably installed during World War Two to prevent over-gauge loads from proceeding to Cliff Common and onto the main line. Just to the right of the stationmaster's house the grounded body of the former guards van can be seen. This had been transformed into a garage for the stationmaster's car, but previously it had a different role in the life of the district, as will be seen later.

(Photo: Ken Hartley Courtesy R. Redman)

Right: No.65677 waits for the shunter to complete his work at Skipwith on 27 April 1954. The two 'Nissen' huts by the station platform and loading dock are visible in the background.

(Photo: J.J. Davies Copyright Historical Model Railway Society)

Left: Class J25 No.65700 shunts at Skipwith on 8 September 1952.

(Photo: W.S. Garth Copyright Rail Archive Stephenson)

Right: Having finished shunting No.65700 prepares to depart with at least one spectator present.
(Photo: W.S. Garth Copyright Rail Archive Stephenson)

Left: No.65714 is halted at Skipwith on 7 April 1956 while the excursion passengers are stretching their legs on the platform. By this time the station was also being used to store timber.

(Photo: J.C. Halliday)

Right: Nearly at the end of the up trip to Cliff Common on 9 January 1965 D2111 reaches Skipwith station.
(Photo: David J. Mitchell)

Left: The platelayers' trolley at Skipwith about which we shall be hearing more later. (Photo: David J. Mitchell)

Right: Skipwith station in February 1966 a year after the closure of the line to Cliff Common. The large fertiliser store, built in 1958, can be seen in the distance. (Photo: David J. Mitchell)

Left: Skipwith station in March 1981 when the station building had been repainted.
(Photo: J.D. Stockwell)

Right: Today the station operates as a self-catering holiday centre with guests staying in three former main line Mark Two coaches. The station building has been restored, and also repainted closer to its original colours. (Photo: J.D. Stockwell)

Cliff Common

Above: Class J25 No.65714 waits to depart from Cliff Common in the late 1950s with the ex-SECR brake van. The former Easingwold coach is in the middle distance.
(Photo: David Lawrence Copyright Colour-Rail BRE2450)

From Skipwith the line crossed the Skipwith Road and then curved south running on the level across Sandy Lane crossing. It then turned south east and descended on a grade of 1 in 330 for a few hundred yards, before running level again for just over half a mile to the level crossing over the A163 to Selby.

Having traversed the crossing, the line fell again on a grade of 1 in 330 for half a mile turning south again to the crossing over South Duffield Road, now known as Greengate Lane. From here the line curved gradually south west for over a mile and a quarter largely on the level until, a quarter of a mile from Cliff Common, there was a slight climb of 1 in 660 on a curve of 836 yard radius. This brought it parallel with the main line.

Cliff Common station of course pre-dated the DVLR, as it was on the former York and North Midland Railway (Y&NMR) line between Selby and Market Weighton, which opened on 1 August 1848. However, when the station at Cliff Common opened is not certain, as it did not appear in the public timetables until late 1851. It was then known as Cliff Common Gate, becoming Cliff Common from 1864.

Originally the line was single track, with Cliff Common station possessing a single platform, but a second platform was added when the line was doubled around 1889. By 1892 the station also possessed a small goods yard on the up (south) side of the line at the Market Weighton end of the station. There was also a siding and headshunt on the down side (see plan). At the Selby end of the station on the up side, there were also two sidings, one of which served a malthouse. By 1909 a second siding had been added on the down side, and a third siding in the up yard, at the Selby end of the station.

When the DVLR was built it effectively took over the site of the sidings on the down side of the NER station. The down platform was widened for DVLR trains and the company built their own station building. A single siding remained on the north side behind the platform, and two new sidings had been added between the DVLR and NER's lines at the Market Weighton end of the station. Connections were also added so that the DVLR metals could be accessed by trains from the NER tracks from either the Selby, or Market Weighton directions. However, in late 1926 the LNER decided to remove the connections, and associated ground frame, from the Market Weighton direction.

In the 1920s the run-round loop, and associated

siding, were removed to provide materials for extra sidings to be laid at Skipwith and elsewhere. The DVLR lines were controlled from a ground frame, originally sited to the north of the run-round loop, but later moved to a central location in the yard.

Passenger traffic to and from Cliff Common does not seem to have been significant, as testified by the fact that most passenger trains only travelled between Layerthorpe and Skipwith. However, its main use was as an interchange for freight with the NER, and subsequently the LNER and BR. This allowed access to Selby and the East Coast main line, as well as the docks at Goole and Hull. Some years after

the end of their passenger services the DVLR station buildings were demolished.

The BR station closed to passengers on 20 September 1954, but remained open for goods. However, the threat of the complete closure of the Market Weighton line was sufficient to persuade the DVLR directors to close the line between Wheldrake and Cliff Common. On 16 January 1965 the last train to use the DVLR station was an RCTS excursion after which the tracks were lifted. The BR line to Market Weighton remained open until the summer of 1965.

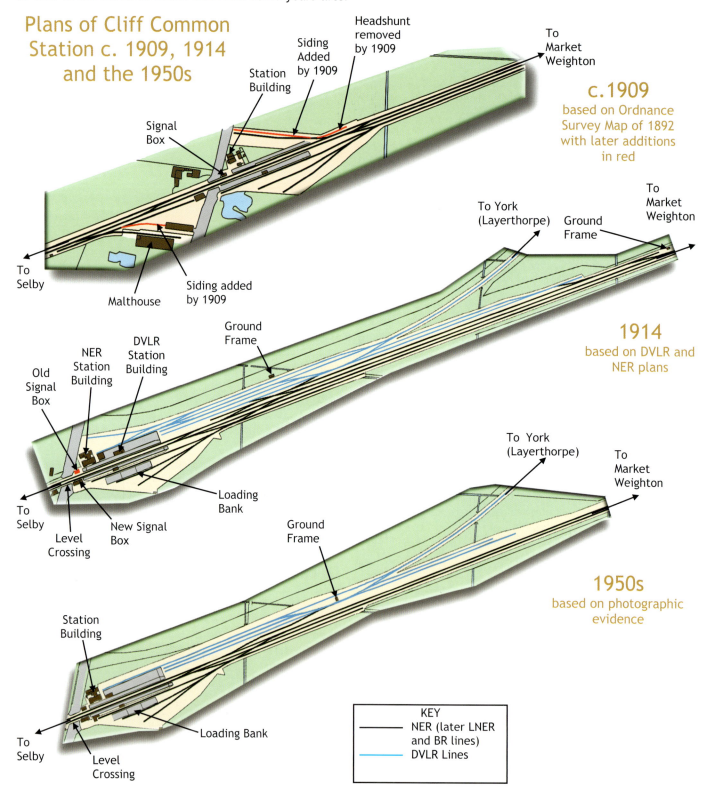

Plans of Cliff Common Station c. 1909, 1914 and the 1950s

c.1909
based on Ordnance Survey Map of 1892 with later additions in red

1914
based on DVLR and NER plans

1950s
based on photographic evidence

KEY
—— NER (later LNER and BR lines)
—— DVLR Lines

Left: Cliff Common station on 19 July 1913 as the opening day train prepares to depart for its return to Layerthorpe. Note the siding nearest the camera and the run-round loop both removed in the 1920s. (Photo: Hanstock Commercial Postcard)

Right: A picture showing the LNER side of the DVLR platform including the other side of the DVLR station building in the 1930s.
(Photo: J.K. Perkin Copyright J.B. Perkin)

Left: LNER class N12 No.2486 waits in the DVLR platform at Cliff Common in the 1930s.
(Photo: J.K. Perkin Copyright J.B. Perkin)

Left: BR class J25 No.65687 is seen at Cliff Common with an interesting mixed train on 9 May 1953. Most of the track layout at this time can be seen in this photo and the one below. Certainly there is a lot of timber stored at the station as part of the government scheme.
(Photo: C.H.A. Townley Copyright Industrial Railway Society)

Right: Looking north east from the DVLR platform at Cliff Common on 27 April 1954. A platelayers' 'sled' appears to be resting against the buffer stops on the left.
(Photo: J.J. Davies Copyright Historical Model Railway Society)

Left: There is still a lot of timber at the site as BR class J25 No. 65677 waits to depart with its train on 4 January 1955.
(Photo: Peter T. Hay)

Right: Conversation at Cliff Common as a couple of enthusiasts chat with the crew of No.65064 as it waits to depart with the down working of the Branch Line special non-stop to Layerthorpe on 17 May 1958.
(Photo: D.A. Kelso)

Above: Having traversed the DVLR from Layerthorpe, Ivatt 2-6-0 No.46409 finally returns to BR metals at Cliff Common on 27 September 1963.
(Photo: David J. Mitchell)

Right: D2111 reaches its destination at Cliff Common on 9 January 1965 with the RCTS special, and pauses beside the ground frame hut before entering the station.
(Photo: David J. Mitchell)

Left: One other well photographed item on the DVLR was this ex-Manchester, Sheffield and Lincolnshire Railway coach, which was stored at Cliff Common.

It was never owned by the DVLR, but was in fact used on the Easingwold Railway. In 1957 it was purchased for preservation and moved to Cliff Common, remaining there until the station closed, after which it was moved to Elvington and kept there. The Railway Preservation Society then acquired it and moved it to Chasewater in 1968, where it has been restored.
(Photo: David J. Mitchell)

Right: The train prepares to depart on the down trip to Layerthorpe on 9 January 1965. The express headcode is being displayed because in theory the train would run non-stop to Layerthorpe. There would be only one more passenger excursion on this section of track before it closed a week later.
(Photo: David J. Mitchell)

Left: Rusting rails at Cliff Common. Just over a year later in February 1966 all the DVLR tracks on the left had been lifted, and only the ground frame hut remained. The main BR tracks were still in place although the line had closed for goods the previous summer.
(Photo: David J. Mitchell)

Locomotives

For most of its life the DVLR 'hired in' locomotives to run its services, initially also with crews, but later they employed their own. There was also a brief spell in the 1920s when the railway purchased its own motive power, but with limited success. It was not to be until 1969 that it would once more buy its own locomotives, and would remain self-sufficient until the line to Dunnington closed.

The First Ten Years

As already stated the railway initially hired in locomotives and crews from the NER. The first engine seen in service was No.1679, which pulled the opening train. This was a 2-2-4 tank locomotive that was usually used to haul the NER Directors' Saloon. It is believed that this was the only time it was used on the line.

Among the first NER locomotives employed regularly on the line were class '398' 0-6-0 tender locomotives.

Above: NER No.1679 hauled the opening train on the DVLR. This locomotive was a unique design being a 2-2-4 tank. It usually only handled light duties such as pulling the NER's Directors' Saloon. It is seen here at Elvington festooned for the festivities.
(Photo: Hanstock Commercial Postcard)

Left: Unfortunately not a view on the DVLR, but nevertheless a NER class '398', No.783 on the turntable at Bradford Foster Square. These were the first class of tender locomotives used on the DVLR.   (Photo: D.J. Williamson Collection)

Below: In 1914 it was agreed with the Ministry that LNER class G5 0-4-4T (previously NER class O) should be used on the line after the accident of 1913. However, it is unclear how long these locos were employed on the DVLR although they were stated as being in use in 1919. Raymond Howden also recalled No.505, seen below at Scarborough, having been used on the line.
(Photo: D.J. Williamson Collection)

These had been designed by Edward Fletcher in 1871, with 325 of the class being built. No.174 was noted in service on the line during the summer of 1913.

However, following the accident of October 1913 (see page 24) it was agreed, after much discussion about axle loadings and coupled wheelbases, that tank locomotives should be used. Following some trials, both the railway and the Ministry pronounced that they were happy that NER class O (later LNER G5) 0-4-4's should be employed. These had been designed by Wilson Worsdell with 110 being built between 1894 and 1901. How long these locomotives continued to be used

Left: This is the only known photograph of the DVLR rail-lorry complete with its purpose-built body. It comes from *The Locomotive* for 15 November 1923. Unfortunately the location is unknown either on the DVLR or, more likely, at the Four-Wheel Drive Co Ltd's factory at Slough. Nevertheless it does show the simple construction of the vehicle, and its lightweight nature that ultimately led to its rejection by the DVLR.

(Photographer Unknown
Courtesy Ian Allan Publishing)

is a matter of conjecture at the present time as there is little information from this period.

The Rail-Lorry

In 1922, with the conclusion of the first working agreement between the NER and the DVLR approaching, Mr Grundy wrote to the MoT. In his letter he stated that the Company was thinking of looking at an alternative to steam power for use on the line, and asking if this would contravene its Light Railway Order.

The following year he wrote again, as the directors had decided to look at some innovative new pieces of equipment that had come onto the market. In fact they were in discussions with The British Four-Wheel Drive Tractor Lorry Super Engineering Co Ltd, which had a factory in Slough. This company produced what essentially were four-wheel drive rail-mounted lorries.

For the DVLR it produced a bespoke rail-truck, which was illustrated in *The Locomotive*. On delivery on 23 October 1923 it was said that when tested 'It hauled five wagons five yards and exploded'. Certainly its early return to the manufacturer on 31 October would seem to support this assertion. However, a document has come to light that paints a slightly different picture.

In reality on the afternoon of 23 October the rail-lorry made a successful round-trip to Cliff Common, hauling over 66 tons at one point. However, the next day it broke down at Dunnington and had to be towed back to Layerthorpe. After repairs it made a run to Dunnington on the Friday hauling over 100 tons on its return. The following Monday (29 October) it made an afternoon run to Cliff Common, with a peak load of 181 tons on the return trip.

By now, though it was becoming clear that the lorry

struggled on greasy rails, despite the provision of sandboxes, and could only reach a top speed of 12 mph with difficulty. This became absolutely apparent when it did its first morning run with a load to Dunnington on Wednesday 31 October. In the end the train had to be divided at Tang Hall Lane bridge, taking 47 minutes to reach Osbaldwick at a speed of 2.5 mph. It was this run that evidently sealed its fate, and the rail-lorry was returned to the manufacturer.

The rail-lorry was 16 ft 2 in long over the headstocks, fitted with a 36 hp four-cylinder petrol engine. It had a four-speed constant mesh gearbox and a Hele-Shaw multiple disc clutch running in oil. The drive was by Cardan shafts to both axles. Theoretically it could achieve 2.6, 4, 8 and 16 mph in either direction, with drum brakes on each of the wheels and the transmission. As can be seen from the photograph it was fitted with a wooden body complete with cab. Despite being less than successful on the DVLR later developments of the type were sold, including one that survived at Dinorwic quarries for many years.

The Railbuses

More successful were the railbuses which the Company bought in 1924. Mr Grundy seems to have been impressed by the railmotors bought by Colonel Stephens for use on the lines with which he was associated. Therefore, two vehicles were purchased for the DVLR in May 1924 at a cost of £1,070.

They were based on Ford 1 ton truck chasses and fitted with bodies manufactured by C.H. Roe of Crossgates, Leeds. Each was fitted with a 22 hp petrol engine with 'Supaphord' gears. An article in *The Locomotive* of 15 January 1915 described the chassis has having been modified for rail use, with such things at 'Timkin' roller bearings, while the wheels had ash spokes and steel tyres.

Right: The railbuses at Layerthorpe. Their lightweight construction is evident in this view. Raymond Howden, who is sitting on the step, was their regular driver. On the left is D. Livingstone, stated to be a trainee driver, while on the right is G. Metcalfe, ganger.
(Photographer Unknown Courtesy Ken Nelson Collection)

Below Left and Right: Part of the original plans for the railbuses.

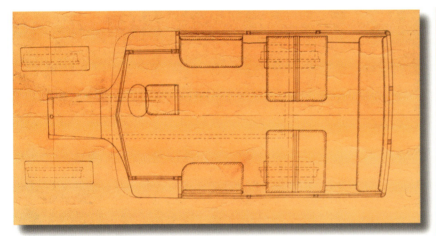

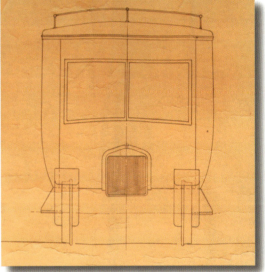

The handbrake had also been modified, so that its operation in one of the buses applied the brakes to both. Another useful addition was that of sandboxes, adhesion being a problem with light vehicles, as the railway had discovered with the rail-lorry. Meanwhile the interiors had sprung seats upholstered in brown leather.

The buses were capable of being run independently, but in order to allow them to operate as single units, turntables were installed at Layerthorpe and Skipwith. Here a running shed for the buses was also constructed. Their livery seems to have been the dark blue used for the first coaches. In service they proved reasonably successful, but the effects of bus competition led to their withdrawal.

After arriving back from their loan to the LNER during the general strike, they were put up for sale in June 1926. They were purchased by the County Donegal Railways Joint Committee for £480, including a spare

Above: The remains of the railbus turntable at Layerthorpe. To the rear left is one of the remaining cattle pens.
(Photo: DVRCo Archive)

Left: The Sentinel takes water at Layerthorpe. Note the absence of the locomotive shed, which in later years would be on the left, but was not built until 1928.
(Photographer Unknown DVRCo Archive)

followed the test mentioned earlier, and was the first introduced into service on a British railway.

The Sentinel (works no.6076) had a vertically mounted boiler which supplied two cylinders, each 6¾ by 9 in, with steam at a pressure of 275 lb. Power was then transmitted to the axles by means of chains and gears, rather than traditional piston and coupling rods, generating 100 hp. It had a wheelbase of 7 ft with 2 ft 6 in diameter driving wheels. When it was loaded with 300 gallons of water, and half a ton of coal, it weighed 22 tons in total. Livery is an interesting question with the locomotive probably being delivered in grey, but subsequently painted green.

Apparently the DVLR found that its daily coal consumption was nine cwt in service, reducing operating costs from 1s 4d for hired locomotives to 8d daily. However, a series of teething problems, plus difficulties in dealing with increased loads, led to its premature end on the DVLR. It was sold to Summerson & Sons Ltd in early 1929 for use at their Albert Hill Foundry in Darlington for £500, before being finally scrapped in 1971.

An Interesting Might-Have-Been

One interesting might-have-been has also come to light from a surviving set of Company minutes from 1927. This was that the LNER offered the DVLR a class J76 locomotive for £600. These was an 0-6-0 tank locomotive, twelve of which were built for the NER from a design by Edward Fletcher between 1881 and 1882. There are no further details of which locomotive was offered, or why the DVLR turned it down.

engine, auxiliary gearbox and magneto. The Donegal just beat Colonel Stephens, who was also keen to acquire them. In Ireland they were adapted for the 3 ft gauge by having the floor level of the passenger body lowered. This not only helped with access from ground level, but also lowered the centre of gravity. They continued in service until withdrawn and scrapped in 1934.

The Sentinel

The third form of motive power the DVLR bought at this time was another pioneering type of locomotive, the 'Super-Sentinel'. This was a radical design of 0-4-0 steam shunting locomotive designed by the Sentinel Waggon Works Ltd at their factory in Shrewsbury. It was purchased by the Company for £1,400 in late spring 1925. This

Right: Another official photo of the Sentinel shunter at Layerthorpe. This view appeared in some of the Sentinel company's advertising.
(Photo: DVRCo Archive)

Right: Despite the accident of 1913 tender locomotives seem to have returned to the DVLR from the 1930s. This is a wartime view of J21 No. 806 at Cliff Common in 1942.
(Right: Ronald Shephard DVRCo Archive)

It is possible that after their recent experiences, the Sentinel was having a broken crankshaft repaired at the time, the directors were nervous of taking on the financial liability as a major expenditure could have crippled the Company. Certainly within the Board there seems to have been a disposition towards the concept of hiring locomotives from the LNER again, and it might well have been this that led to the offer being declined.

Hiring Again

A new hiring agreement was made with the LNER in 1928, at what the Board felt were favourable rates. LNER locomotives had had to be hired in on an 'ad-hoc' basis during the Sentinel's breakdowns, but now once again they provided the motive power for the weekday goods services.

Among the locomotives working on the line in the late 1920s and 1930s were class N12 0-6-2 tank locomotives. These were designed for the Hull and Barnsley Railway by Matthew Stirling, with nine being built by Kitsons in 1901. A majority of the class were noted on the DVLR during this period, particularly Nos. 2483, 2485, 2486, 2488, 2490 2491 and 2492.

However, there is an interesting footnote to this in that the axle loading of the N12's was 16.75 tons, above the line's rating at the time. In fact, the permitted axle loading was not increased sufficiently for the N12's to be used until 1938, officially.

Another class of engine noted on the line was the G6 class of 0-4-4 tank locomotive. No.416 was seen at work on the line in 1928. They were designed by Edward Fletcher for the NER and introduced from 1874, with a total of 124 being constructed. In the late 1930s Nos. 1645 and 1650 of class N9 0-6-4 tanks, another ex-NER class of which twenty were built in 1893 and 1894, were also in operation on the line.

Tender locomotives also made a re-appearance during this time. No.1804, a member of the LNER class J21, being noted in use. It was an 0-6-0 tender locomotive, designed by T.W. Worsdell, one of 201 that were built between 1886 and 1894. Whether formal approval had been gained for the re-introduction of tender locos is not known, or it might have simply been a case of what the Ministry didn't know wouldn't worry them!

During the war there is little doubt that a greater variety of locomotives operated on the DVLR. However, the restrictions of wartime mean that relatively little is

known of precisely which classes were employed on the line, other than a note that some 'MoT types' were used. A class J21 0-6-0 tender locomotive No.806 was noted in a photograph of 1942 (see above), while a class J71 0-6-0 tank locomotive No. 449 also operated on the line during the conflict (see below). The J71s were another Worsdell design of which 120 were constructed by the NER between 1886 and 1895.

Right: Another 1942 view, this time of J71 No.449 at Layerthorpe.
(Photo: Ronald Shephard Courtesy West Sussex Record Office)

Left: Class J25 No.65714 on 7 June 1960 the final months of steam freight working on the DVLR.
(Photo: V. Nutton
Courtesy Travel Lens Photographic)

The End of Locomotive Hiring

In 1969 the DVLR once more took the decision to buy its own locomotives. As a result, two class 04 ex-BR diesel shunters were purchased. The first, D2298, was built in 1960 and spent most of its working life in East Anglia before being sent to Gateshead, where it was withdrawn before being sold to the DVLR in April 1969. After arrival at Layerthorpe it was repainted in Minerva Grey, with black and red panels, plus the obligatory 'wasp' warning stripes. It was given the number 'one'.

Diesel No.2 was ex-BR D2245, which had been built in 1956, and was purchased in May 1969 having served at Goole docks. Both locomotives were fitted with Gardner 8L3 engines generating 204 hp, with mechanical transmission. A third 04 was also purchased from BR, ex-D2329 being bought for spares, and came partly dismantled from Peter Wood and Co of Ecklington, Sheffield, but with no power unit.

DVLR, later DVR, No.2 lasted in service until May 1978 when it was sold to the Shackerstone Railway. It was

Post-War and Nationalisation

After the war the DVLR continued to hire locomotives. Going into the 1950s class J25 0-6-0 tender locomotives became synonymous with the line. Nos. 65687, 65700 and 65714 were noted in use, with No.65714 probably the last steam locomotive to be hired from BR. They were designed by Wilson Worsdell, with 120 being built between 1898 and 1902, and lasted in service until 1963. They were not fitted with vacuum brakes, and therefore were suited only for goods work.

For the passenger excursions generally vacuum braked class J21s, again 0-6-0 tender engines, were employed. Noted on the line during this time were class J21 Nos. 65064 and 65078. In addition, there were also occasional appearances by other locomotives, such as the Ivatt 4MT which was involved in the Mustard Gas trains from Cottingwith. Class J24 No.65619 was also seen in 1950.

Dieselisation

With the withdrawal of many steam locomotives, including those of the J21 and J25 classes, in 1961 diesels took over operation of the line. Shunters from what became the class 03 fleet were used. D2103 and D2110 being noted on the DVLR during this period. The following year a class 04 D2269 was seen in use, before class 03's became the normal locomotives employed up until 1969. Among those seen on the line were D2054, D2111, D2112, D2113 and D2122.

Right: A different view of J25 No.65714 as it stands at Cliff Common on 7 June 1960.
(Photo: V. Nutton Courtesy Travel Lens Photographic)

Left and Below: The DVLR bought two class 04 diesel shunters from BR in 1969. D2298 became DVLR No.1 which is seen at Dunnington on the left on 27 May 1972. Meanwhile D2245 became DVLR No.2 and is seen below at Layerthorpe on 25 February 1970. Interestingly both locomotives were lettered for the Derwent Valley Railway, the word Light being omitted. This was despite the official name change not occurring until 1973.

(Left: David J. Mitchell
Below: J.H. Meredith)

Left: Later DVR No.1 was repainted into green and named *Lord Wenlock*. It is seen at Layerthorpe on 18 May 1977.

(Photo: David J. Mitchell)

replaced by a Fowler 0-4-0 diesel mechanical, works no.4210142, built in 1958, and originally supplied to the Ministry of Fuel and Power at Oxspring. It was purchased by the DVR from the British Pipeline Agency Ltd of Rawcliffe Bridge near Goole.

When it arrived at Layerthorpe it was painted in a variant of lined LNER green and named *Claude Thompson*. No.1 was similarly repainted being named *Lord Wenlock*. After the ending of railway services on the line to Dunnington,

No.1 *Lord Wenlock* was sold to the Buckinghamshire Railway Centre in October 1982. Meanwhile *Claude Thompson* went to L. Clancey and Sons, the scrap merchants at Murton, before being sold to Coopers (Metals) Ltd at Sheffield. Later it was a static exhibit outside Marple and Gillot, who had been responsible for lifting the line from Cliff Common in 1965.

Meanwhile of course the DVR had acquired and sold another steam locomotive ex-BR No. 69023, which had been originally built by BR in 1951 to the design of the former LNER J72 class of 0-6-0 tank locomotives. By 1964 No.69023 had been taken into BR's departmental stock as No.59, initially based at Gateshead, but later at North Blyth and Heaton for de-icing duties. It was purchased from BR for preservation by Ronald Ainsworth in 1966 and sent to the Keighley and Worth Valley Railway (KWVR).

On the KWVR it was painted in NER livery, even though it was never in NER service, and named *Joem* in memory of Mr Ainsworth's parents. Initially the DVR hired *Joem* for the 1977 season, but later purchased it. However, when in 1979 the company decided to end steam services a clause in the purchase contract was enacted whereby the Ainsworth family had first refusal on any further sale.

As a result of this Ronald Ainsworth's son Paul purchased

the loco and it was put into storage at the NRM. Later it was put up for auction at Sotheby's on 4 December 1981, but was not sold. During 1982 several preserved railways showed an interest, but there were no takers. Happily by the end of 1982 the loco had been sold to the North Eastern Locomotive Preservation Group for £10,250. It has since seen service on several preserved railways since, most recently on the Wensleydale Railway in North Yorkshire.

There was, though, one other locomotive associated with the DVR in its later years. This was a Fowler 0-4-0 diesel-mechanical, works no.4100005, built in 1947 originally for Reed Board Mills (Colthorp) Ltd at Thatcham, and named *Churchill*. It was purchased by Yorkshire Grain Driers Ltd in 1971 for shunting duties at Dunnington. After the line to Dunnington was closed, it was bought by the DVR and put up for sale with the rest of their locomotives in September 1982. However, no buyer was found, and so instead it was presented to the Yorkshire Museum of Farming at Murton in September 1983. *Churchill* is now based on the preserved Derwent Valley Light Railway at the museum site.

Above: *Joem* at the buffer stops at Dunnington in August 1979.
(Photo: J.D. Stockwell)

Right: *Claude Thompson* with *Lord Wenlock* on the last day of DVR operations. (Photo: N. Beilby)

Below: *Churchill* at Dunnington in August 1979.
(Photo: J.D. Stockwell)

Rolling Stock

Most items of rolling stock that ran on the DVLR belonged to other companies or railways. They were used to transport goods and materials to and from the wider network. The DVLR did though own some items of rolling stock for their own essentially internal use, either for passengers, goods or engineering supplies.

These were sadly infrequently photographed, and there is little information as to their origins etc. However, these pages attempt to summarise the known information on the DVLR's rolling stock, starting with the passenger coaches. Even here there are conflicting references, but it is hoped that some mysteries might be solved.

Left: In the photograph of the opening train there are two carriages, a four-wheel brake composite, and a six-wheel third. These were ex-NER coaches. The six-wheeled third is a 30 ft third probably of 1880s vintage. Meanwhile the brake composite is a modified NER diagram 19 six-wheel brake third also built in the 1880s. This has had the centre pair of wheels removed and the centre compartment 'up-graded' to first, although it is unknown how much had been done to justify the new classification. The mix of four-wheel and six-wheel stock has led to some confusion over the years.

(Photo: Hanstock Commercial Postcard)

Right: The brake composite probably in Layerthorpe yard. Originally the coaches were painted dark blue with gold lettering, but at a later stage were repainted brown. In 1916 the two third class compartments were changed to second class, however, by the looks of this photograph this was achieved by taking the numbers off of the doors!

In the photo above the coaches appear to have fittings for gas lighting in their roofs, but these had disappeared in the photo to the right, and a dynamo has been fitted. This suggests the coaches were converted to electric lighting during their time on the DVLR.

(Photo: Rail Archive Stephenson)

Above: By the end of 1913 the DVLR owned three carriages. The two seen in the opening train and another, acquired subsequently. This was originally an NER diagram 15 32 ft six-wheel third, but with the centre compartment converted to a first for service on the DVLR. All the carriages had Westinghouse braking, and taken together they had a total seating capacity of 130.

They were all used on the last regular passenger train to Skipwith, and then put up for sale. Early in 1928 they were sold to the Darlington Rolling Stock Company for £75, and are seen here at the Darlington Co's sidings at Eryholme Junction. Here the bodies were on sale for £17 10s each plus carriage. The sale of the coaches meant that when the DVLR started to operate excursion trains again in summer 1928, they had to hire in carriages from the LNER.

(Photo: D.J. Williamson Collection)

Left: The original return to the Ministry from the railway indicated that they had eight open wagons for loads between eight and twelve tons. Two were used in the opening train, and one of these is seen in the photograph to the left. This an ex-NER four-plank wagon built to diagram C2.
(Photo: Hanstock Commercial Postcard)

Right: A two-plank dropside wagon (No.3) in DVLR livery in 1935. This was another ex-NER wagon built to diagram B1. Probably many of the open wagons were used for ballast and other permanent way materials, although here it does seem to be carrying some kind of commercial load.
(Photo: Ronald Shephard
Courtesy West Sussex Record Office)

Left: The DVLR originally owned two cattle trucks, only adding a third in 1923. As this photo is of DVLR No.3 a reasonable deduction was that it was photographed around the time of its arrival on the line. This helps in the dating of the other 'official' photographs that are part of the same set found in the Company archives.

Once again this was an ex-NER vehicle, built to diagram K1, but modified with oil axle boxes. More cattle wagons were added during the 1920s. They were possibly the only DVLR owned vehicles to travel off the line after the end of passenger services. This is because there was a weekly cattle train that ran into York cattle market in the mid to late 1930s.
(Photo: DVLRS/YMF Archive)

Right: In February 1966 David Mitchell photographed two wagons in the yard at Wheldrake. The nearest one appears to be one of the DVLR's own wagons, which were then painted green.

In 1928 the Railway owned seven opens and six cattle trucks, along with the travelling crane. The opens included two ex-LNER 10.5 ton ballast wagons bought at the end of 1927 for £16 each. By 1948 the stock had dropped to one open wagon, four cattle trucks and the crane. In 1960 there were three opens, one cattle truck and the crane. Then in 1972 it was two opens, one covered van, and a crane.
(Photo: David J. Mitchell)

Left: The DVLR had one ex-NER brake van when it opened in 1913, possibly it was purchased the year before for the initial goods service. It is seen here at the back of the opening train departing from Cliff Common. This van appears to be of the type known as a NER V1/2, built at Shildon, mostly in the late 1880s and early 1890s. They were reckoned to be re-builds of earlier York, Newcastle and Berwick Railway vans. However, how long it lasted in service is unknown, as it seems to have been replaced by the one in the photo below.
(Photo: Hanstock Commercial Postcard)

Right: The second brake van used by the DVLR was a NER type V1/1 with horizontal planking. These were based on a design by the York and North Midland Railway, and were built at York in the 1890s. Unfortunately its date of acquisition by the DVLR is unknown, but it was taken out of use in 1927. The body was purchased by the porter-in-charge at Skipwith, Henry Howden. It was transported to the station by rail, and was wheeled to a site beside the stationmaster's house. After its arrival it served a number of purposes, here it seems to be full of straw bedding, perhaps a home for the ducks?
(Photo: Lavinia Nelson née Howden)

Left and below: The third ex-NER brake van was purchased in 1925. This was of the type built by the NER and known as V1/3, which were built from 1896 until 1902. These were narrower than the other two V1 types with a width of 7 ft 6 ins as opposed to 8 ft, and also had vertical planking. Like the other vans it has not proved possible at this time to determine which number this van carried in NER service, although it was built at Shildon in 1900. It is seen left at Layerthorpe on 17 May 1958. (Left Photo: D.A. Kelso)

Right: It remained in use until 1947, when it in turn was replaced by the ex-SECR six-wheel brake. For many years it was used as a store at Layerthorpe, being stood at the end of the siding opposite the platform, as the photographs above and to the right show, the latter being taken in September 1958.
(Photo: David J. Mitchell)

Left: The four-wheel ex-NER brake van was replaced by the SECR six-wheel brake van, purchased from the Southern Railway in 1946. It is seen here at Layerthorpe on 17 May 1958. This had been built in 1905 as No.719, and was unusual in that it had a 'bird-cage' look-out in the roof and side ducket for the guard. One of the van's last duties prior to its sale to the DVLR was being used as a cleansing van for the Air Raid Precautions. This was when it was based at Bricklayer's Arms loco department.

The van had a large luggage compartment, which was useful for accommodating the enthusiasts who travelled over the line. It also had a series of pigeonholes which were used for documents and messages to and from the stations on the line. In 1967 it was sold for preservation by the Southern Locomotive Preservation Co, and was eventually moved to the Bluebell Railway in February 1972. Today the van is awaiting restoration.

(Photo: D.A. Kelso)

Right: The SECR brake van was replaced by a four-wheeled LNER Pigeon Brake van No.70250. As its name implies, this was one of 45 similar vehicles constructed which could be attached to passenger trains for the transportation of racing pigeons. When they reached their destination the pigeons could then be released and race back to their lofts.

No.70250 was originally built in 1930 and carried the number 6854 up until 1946 when it was re-numbered 70250. It remained in service with BR until sold to the DVLR in 1966. Here it lasted in service until the mid-1970s, when it was sold to the Llangollen Railway. They converted it into a saloon coach for disabled children.

(Photo: H.C. Casserley)

Left: The piece of original DVLR equipment which lasted the longest was the travelling crane. Unfortunately despite its longevity very little is known about it. It was built by I'Anson & Co, Darlington and was capable of lifting a load of 3.5 tons. The date and manner of its disposal is also something of a mystery, with the last known photos being at Wheldrake in 1968. It is seen here in Wheldrake yard lifting a cultivator on 27 April 1954.

(Photo: J.J. Davis Copyright HMRS)

Left: The original travelling crane was replaced by a second. This was former BR DE902165 built by Cowans Sheldon in 1892, works no.1764. It does not seem to have lasted long on the DVLR, but was seen at Layerthorpe in July 1974. This photograph being taken in November 1973. There was also a match truck, former BR DE300445 built at Wolverton in 1929.

(Photo: J.C. Dean)

Right: By the late 1970s a third crane, a Coles KL15 mounted on a 24 ft flat wagon, was in service. It is seen here at Layerthorpe on 12 March 1979. In September 1981 it was listed as being for sale along with three further flat wagons, an ex-GWR 12 ton van no.125222, and a steel box van body, but nothing is known of their disposal.

(Photo: R.R. Darsley)

In the late 1970s the DVR did own passenger carriages again in the form of three ex-BR Mark One coaches. These were Second Corridor E24804; First Corridor E13043 and Brake Composite E21100. After the end of the steam service they were sold to the North Yorkshire Moors Railway.

Left: However, later the DVR leased some bulk grain wagons from Procor to transport dried grain from Dunnington to Scotland. They are seen here by the plant at Dunnington.

(Photographer Unknown DVRCo Archive)

People

Of course while one might look at the locomotives and rolling stock, as well as all the infrastructure of a railway, it is the people that make it work. On the DVLR there were different groups of people who all played their part in keeping the line going. First there was the Board of Directors, who gave the general direction to the Company. Responsible for the day-to-day operations was the general manager, but then it was the staff including stationmasters, porters, drivers, firemen and track workers who made it happen on the ground.

The Board of Directors

By the time the line opened on 19 July 1913 the Board of Directors consisted of: Lord Deramore of Heslington Hall (Chairman); Sir Robert Walker of Sand Hutton; Claude Thompson (Land agent for the Escrick estate); Mr Wilfrid Thomson of York and Mr Eric Geddes (Deputy general manager of the NER). The first four were to serve for many years, joined by another long-time director Lt-Col Dunnington-Jefferson.

Above: A photo some of the directors along with visitors from the LNER taken in 1946 at Layerthorpe. In the picture standing left to right: Mjr S.W. Harland (sec. DVLR); Mr J. Taylor Thompson (engineer, LNER, York); Mr S.T. Burgoyne (passenger manager LNER N.E. area); Mr C.M. Steadman (Loco. running superintendent LNER N.E. area); Mr S.J. Reading (general manager DVLR); Mr R. Richardson (director DVLR).
Sitting left to right: Mr P.Gibb (LNER general manager, N.E. area); Sir J.A. Dunnington-Jefferson (vice-chairman DVLR); Mr C.M. Jenkin Jones (LNER divisional general manager, N.E. Area; Mr C.W. Thompson (chairman DVLR); Mr E.M. Rutter (LNER superintendent N.E. area); Sir Ivo Thomson (director DVLR). (Photo: *The York Press*)

In 1936 Lord Deramore passed away and Claude Thompson succeeded him as chairman. Mr Thompson held the post throughout World War Two and the 1950s until 1961. He was described as a man of great energy, even scrambling up a pile of rubble at the age of eighty. Certainly it can be said that if any one person embodied the DVLR it was him, for without his efforts it is doubtful that the line would have been built, or lasted as long as it did. In total he served the railway for nearly sixty years.

By 1953 the directors were Claude Thompson (chairman); Lt-Col Dunnington-Jefferson; Colin Forbes-Adam; Sir Ivo Wilfrid Thomson; Richard Richardson, who was connected to Glossops, and Edward Arkle (Commercial superintendent of the British Transport Commission). The first three continued to serve as directors into the 1960s. In 1961 there was another change in chairmanship with Lt-Col Dunnington-Jefferson taking on the role, but in reality there was a fundamental change about to take place.

Originally the directors were composed largely of the local landowners who were also shareholders. They were primarily involved because they wanted the railway to benefit their estates, tenant farmers, as well as the rest of the local community. Therefore, they ran it not necessarily on a purely commercial basis, indeed for many years the directors guaranteed the Company overdraft.

In the 1960s this began to change, with the name Roy Cook appearing as one of the directors from 1962. He was then owner of Yorkshire Grain Driers Ltd, and was a businessman first and foremost. One can detect his increasing influence as the decade progressed, and it is no surprise that he succeeded Lt-Col Dunnington-Jefferson as chairman in 1970. By now he had sold his interest in the grain driers, and so he also became managing director, working with the general manager, Jim Acklam.

There is no doubt that Roy Cook was an entrepreneur, but he was also mindful of the responsibilities of running a railway. This is borne out by the quantity of correspondence between himself and the MoT during his

Left: Mr Roy Cook seen at Layerthorpe in 1976.
(Photo: DVRCo Archive)

tenure. He also brought people in with specific expertise, such as John Bullock, who had property development experience, and became a director in the 1970s.

Roy Cook was not adverse to trying new things, such as the steam passenger service, if it had potential to make money for the Company. It is said that at the conclusion of one directors' meeting Roy told them that they would have to find a new venue, as the 'Portakabin' they were then occupying had been sold, and was due to be removed! Roy was to remain the chairman until 1985.

Serving the Board of Directors there were also the company secretaries. The first was Mr H.W. Badger, who was responsible for much of the acquisition of the land for the railway. He was succeeded by Mr W.H. Simpson, who served from 1935 to 1944, with Mr G.H. Foote acting in the post until 1946. Mjr S. Harland then took over, remaining in the position until 1973. Finally David Blackburn took on the role in 1973 until the takeover of the Company.

General Managers

Throughout its life, the DVLR had only five chairmen and four general managers. Initially Claude Thompson acted as managing director, overseeing the Company until construction of the line was underway.

Mr. J. L. Clewes,
General Manager, Derwent Valley Light Railway.

(Photo: *North Eastern Railway Magazine*)

In mid-1912 Mr J.L. Clewes was appointed as the first general manager, to prepare the railway for opening. He had worked for the Midland Railway for many years, his last post being general inspector to the chief goods officer. However, he was not to remain in the post long, departing for Ireland in mid-1914 to manage the Londonderry and Lough Swilly Railway (L&LSR).

It is not easy to gain an impression of why his management of the DVLR did not last long. Perhaps, though, some clue comes from the fact that he only lasted at the L&LSR until September 1916. He departed when the L&LSR brought in someone over him, because, it was reported, his management 'lacked vigour'.

He was replaced at the DVLR by Mr W.T. Grundy, who had also started work on the Midland Railway, in his case at Bingley in 1891. His previous appointment prior to coming to the DVLR was being in charge of the joint Midland and London and North Western Railways' depot at Morecambe.

The words that seem to sum up Grundy's tenure were economy, and technological innovation. In particular he was keen on any technological innovation that could lead to economy. He was responsible, for example, for the installation of electric lighting in Layerthorpe yard, and was also the driving force behind the acquisition of the rail-lorry, railbuses and Sentinel shunter.

However, he appears to have had a weakness in staff relations, and also in trying to generate more traffic on the railway. For example, the failure to pay the staff at the same rates as their main line colleagues led to the industrial problems of 1919. He also seems to have not recognised the importance of simple things, such as holding Staff Dinners, to help building relationships.

In marketing too, his approach seemed to be to either raise revenue, or reduce costs, rather than increase market share. His decision to 'upgrade' the passenger

Above: Taken just before W.T. Grundy left the DVLR, this view shows him on the left, with Mr W.J. Privett (Goods, later chief, clerk), and future general manager S.J. Reading.
(Photo: Courtesy *The Railway Magazine* August 1927)

People

Left: Mr S.J. Reading pictured at Layerthorpe station in the early 1960's. (Photo: N. Coulthard)

1927, here he said: '..provided the confidence of the men can be restored, they will gradually break off their relationship with the NUR'. One suspects though that he viewed this, rightly or wrongly, as a secondary benefit, rather than a primary motive.

Certainly during his tenure there was very much a family feel to the DVLR. Employees were even encouraged to make suggestions for the better running of the railway. On the issue of pay too, there are no further reports of disputes. Indeed in 1942 one correspondent stated that the staff had just received a 10% pay rise without asking for it. It is also said that during Reading's managership he only ever sacked one employee.

His work with the farmers has already been noted. He realised that simple changes in operating practices and facilities could bring good returns. These included the placing of goods wagons on the main line overnight, the provision of extra sidings, delivery services etc. Having an instinct for an opportunity, it was Reading who re-instated the passenger excursions and started the 'blackberry' specials. These not only provided revenue, but also publicity.

It is little surprise that the first part of his tenure saw the

coaches to second class, with the corresponding fare increase being a case in point. The railbuses too with their limited capacity and uncomfortable ride, would surely have been a deterrent to some potential passengers. He did, though, begin the practice of leasing out some of the Company property, such as the yard at Osbaldwick.

When the passenger service ended he proposed to dispense with a guard, stationmaster and a platelayer. However, after the intervention of the National Union of Railwaymen (NUR) once more, it was agreed to retain the stationmaster. In order to pay for this the rest of the staff went on short-time working.

Towards the end of his time as well there seem to have been health issues, as noted in the protracted correspondence with the Ministry over the railbuses. Nevertheless, when he left at the end of 1926 he took up the post of manager of the Liverpool Overhead Railway, a position he was to hold for several years. His successor was Mr Sydney J. Reading, who had been his assistant for a number of years having originally been a clerk to Claude Thompson.

There seems to have been a contrast between these two men. Reading was obviously a 'people' person. After being promoted to acting general manager, he called a meeting of all staff, where he stated that there was an 'urgent need for a better feeling of co-operation and team spirit than had been shown in the past'. He also worked to re-instate full-time working. As he was being paid only £400 a year for the post, as opposed to Grundy's £650, it is obvious where some of the money to make this possible came from. He also reinstated the annual Staff Dinner in 1928, which further improved relationships.

He did, however, appear to have had an ulterior motive. This is witnessed by a statement he made to the Board in

Above: Jim Acklam pictured on his retirement in September 1984. (Photo: *The York Press*)

Company overdraft turned into a credit by 1942. Through the war, as has been seen, many opportunities arose to aid not only the war effort, but also the Company bank balance. During the 1950s as well he maintained the line, again with an entrepreneurial spirit that took advantage of any chance to increase revenue.

When he retired on 31 December 1963, he left a railway that was very different from the one he had inherited. His love for the line was also clear in the history that he wrote of the railway, on which much of our current knowledge is based.

He was succeeded by Jim Acklam, who later with Roy Cook, was to take the railway into a new era. Jim Acklam had started as a clerk on the DVLR, before rising to assistant manager and then manager.

The world was changing rapidly, and the fact that Acklam and Cook managed to keep the railway running as long as they did is a tribute to their partnership. Sadly, however, it was to be the time of gradual retrenchment and closure.

Jim Acklam obviously wasn't adverse to innovation, and his time of course did witness the steam revival, as well as other moves to generate traffic. However, the factors that ultimately led to operations ceasing on progressively more sections of the line, and its final closure, were beyond his control. He remained in charge until effectively all DVR operations ceased, retiring in 1984.

Operational Staff

The initial operational staff of the railway consisted of stationmasters, porters, crossing-keepers and permanent way workers. Of course when the railway began to provide loco crews this was extended to drivers and firemen.

Stationmasters and Porters

When the line opened the stationmasters were: Mr J.W. Steel (Layerthorpe), Mr A.W. Wilkinson (Osbaldwick and Murton), Mr W.J. Privett (Dunnington Halt and Dunnington), Mr H.J. Silke (Elvington), Mr R. Gilbank (Wheldrake), Mr F. Dearnley (Cottingwith and Thorganby), Mr A. Teasdale (Skipwith) and Mr W.J.B. Brown (Cliff Common). They were paid 25 shillings (£1.25) per week.

Later some of the stationmasters were replaced with porters-in-charge, as an economy measure. The remaining stationmasters taking on overall responsibility for a number of stations. When Mr Reading took over as general manager he got the then stationmaster at Layerthorpe, Mr Cartledge, to undertake some of the goods account work, so that his 'time will then be fully occupied'.

It also seemed that the stationmasters, and porters-in-charge, could also run their own coal business from the stations. Jim Acklam, when he was general manager, also had his own coal business at Layerthorpe. He even sold coal to at least one of the directors in the 1970s.

Sadly we do not have a full list of all the stationmasters and porters through the years, but in some cases these posts were handed down through the generations. For example, at Elvington there were three generations of the Handley family who worked there. Harold Handley became porter-in-charge in succession to his father in 1921, being promoted to stationmaster in 1928. He remained in post for thirty-two years, before his son, Sidney Handley, took over. Even Sidney's son was to enter railway service, although in his case it was with British Railways.

There were several others who were long-time employees of the Company. Mr W.J. Privett, for example, the first stationmaster at Dunnington and later chief clerk of the Company, retired in April 1946. He not only served 33 years on the DVLR, but had 20 years of previous railway services, having started work for the London and South Western Railway, and later the Mid-Suffolk Light Railway. Herbert Balderson was reported in 1952 as still working at Elvington, having originally helped build the line. Frank Stabler, who again started with the Company in 1913, was porter-in-charge at Wheldrake in 1954.

Right: Exchange at Layerthorpe between stationmaster Hockley and guard Arthur Todd. Arthur Todd was the son of the long-time porter-in charge at Dunnington, R.A. Todd.
(Photo: Copyright Transport Treasury)

Left: The crew of LNER class N12 No.2485 pose for the camera at Skipwith station in the 1930s. On the left is driver Jack Ratlidge with fireman Duncan Livingstone on the right.
(Photo: Lavina Nelson née Howden)

Below: Left to Right Fireman William Watson, guard Arthur Todd and Driver Bill Leeman in the cab of locomotive No.65714 at Thorganby on 27 June 1957.
(Photo: B. Connell Copyright Photos From The Fifties)

Below: Ken Bell, the DVR's last driver, at the controls of one of the diesel shunters.
(Photo: R.R. Darsley)

Drivers and Firemen

Originally the NER supplied both locomotives and crews for the DVLR. Later this changed, particularly when the DVLR acquired its own motive power. One of the first drivers for the DVLR was Raymond Howden, who drove the railbuses and later the Sentinel. He was succeeded by Jack Ratlidge, whose fireman in 1937 was H. Cooper, and in 1947 S. Eastwood.

In the 1950s Bill Leeman was the driver. He was succeeded by his fireman, William Watson, who drove the last train from Wheldrake in 1968. The railway's last driver was Ken Bell, who drove for the DVLR from 1967 up until the end of the DVR.

Guards

As for most of the railway's life there was only a single goods train operating, the number of guards was limited, with station staff sometimes being employed in the role to cover sickness or holidays. For a long time the regular guard was Walter Gamble, but in 1952 Arthur Todd took on the duty.

Platelayers

When the line opened the contractors, Pethick & Dix, were responsible for the maintenance of the permanent way for the first year. After this the railway employed one ganger, two sub gangers, and six platelayers, the latter being paid at 15 shillings a week.

These were divided into two gangs one, based at Skipwith, covered the line from Cliff Common to Wheldrake. The other was based at Layerthorpe to cover the rest of the line. However, the platelayers could also be called upon to work at the other end of the line, and also at the stations. Therefore, one of the prime requirements, certainly in the 1940s, was that members of the permanent way gangs should be able to cycle. This

Left: The permanent way gang in action at Wheldrake in November 1947, left to right they are Frank Wood, Les Richardson, Phil Heselwood, Ned Jackson, and Dick Howden.

(Photo: *The York Press*)

line from Layerthorpe to Wheldrake. However, they were now given luxury transport in the form of a Company van to get them from one site to another.

Crossing Keepers

Another group of people who contributed to the railway were the crossing keepers. Most of the stations had been built next to road crossings, so that the station staff could operate the crossing gates. However, there were originally seven other gated crossings. These were at Murton and Osbaldwick Road; Sledmere; Elvington Brickyard; Broad Highway; South Moor Lane; Selby Road and South Duffield Road.

was in order for them to get to the places they were needed.

They were also expected to do other tasks on the railway as required, such as loading and unloading goods at the stations. This was particularly true at the harvest time for various crops. Arthur Richmond, who was a platelayer on the line in the 1940s, recalls often being required to go to Elvington or Dunnington stations to help load potatoes and sugar beet.

Originally many of the platelayers were previously farm, or other manual, labourers. However, for some this was the first step on the ladder to other things. For example, Bill Leeman and William Watson started work on the DVLR on the permanent way gang, but eventually became drivers. Others too either rose up the ranks at the DVLR, or transferred to one of the main line companies.

Here houses were provided for the crossing keepers. Initially, when the passenger services were running, there would be a number of trains a day to attend to. However, in latter years there was only one train in each direction. Therefore, it is probably fair to say that the crossing keepers were not overworked! During the steam service there was a mobile gatekeeper who drove ahead of the train to open the gates. In later years the train crews did the job for themselves.

As the length of line reduced, so did the number of staff. In 1947 the railway had 33 employees, but by 1960 this had been reduced to 23. Following the closure of the Cliff Common section it became 13, and by 1973 it was only 8.

As already mentioned during the war extra maintenance of the permanent way was required and labour was short. Therefore, Italian prisoners of war were brought in, twenty starting in May 1944 at the York end, and a further twenty based at Skipwith from June. Later, after the Italians were repatriated at the end of the war, they were replaced by German prisoners of war.

After the closure of the line between Wheldrake and Cliff Common the numbers of staff were reduced, with several porters and platelayers being made redundant. The remaining permanent way workers were reorganised into one gang covering the

Right: The platelayers' van at Layerthorpe on 2 October 1974.

(Photo: R.R. Darsley)

Below: Platelayer H.W. Watson (left) assists porter-in-charge Mr F. Stabler at Wheldrake.

Below: Layerthorpe stationmaster Mr W. Hockley (right) and acting guard Sidney Handley in discussion.

A Snapshot In Time

In November 1947 a photographer from *The Yorkshire Herald* travelled the line taking pictures of the railway and its staff. Although not the best quality these images capture just a moment in time on the DVLR.

(Photos: Courtesy *The York Press*)

Above: Porter R. Andrew (left) with porter-in-charge Mr R.A. Todd at Dunnington.

Above: Father and son at Skipwith porter-in-charge Henry Howden (right) and Eric Howden (left).

Below: Platelayer Ned Jackson.

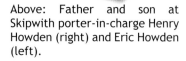

Above: Guard Handley delivers water to the Tindall family at Dunnington Halt.

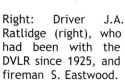
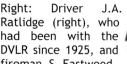

Right: Driver J.A. Ratlidge (right), who had been with the DVLR since 1925, and fireman S. Eastwood.

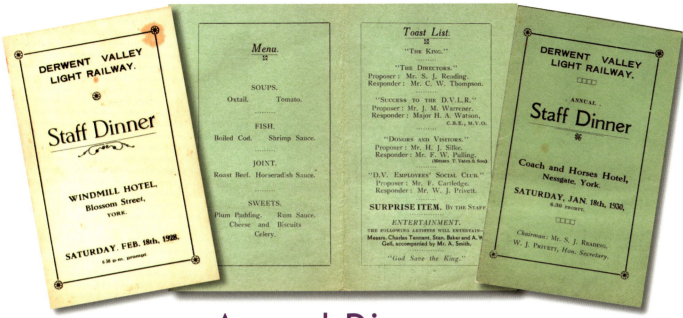

Annual Dinners

In February 1928 the first Staff Dinner since 1913 was held, after which they became an annual event. They even attracted the attention of the local newspaper cartoonist in 1935 (Below). One wonders, though, what the staff's surprise item was in 1930 (Above).

J.D. Stockwell
Collection

Right: There were also staff outings, such as the one on the right, which is ironically being undertaken by coach. At the the left hand end of the front row are Lavinia, Eric and Mabel Howden. Sydney Reading is in the centre of the group.
   (Photo: Lavinia Nelson Collection)

Life At Skipwith Station

For most of its life, one family was responsible for running Skipwith station. Henry Howden, was porter-in-charge there for 43 years before handing the post on to his son Eric. Henry Howden's grandson, Ken Nelson, spent many summers at the station. He, along with his mother Lavinia, have given us an insight into life at the station in the 1930s and 40s with photos from the family album.

(All photos, except where noted, from the Nelson Family Collection, most by Lavinia Nelson née Howden)

Above: Henry and Mabel Howden at Skipwith. Henry had started on the DVLR as a porter at Thorganby, but when the opportunity arose he moved to Skipwith as porter-in-charge, a post he was to hold for 43 years. He and Mabel married when Henry went to Skipwith and they moved into the stationmaster's house. Here they had three children Eric, Lavinia and Richard.

(Photo: Ronald Shephard
Courtesy West Sussex Record Office)

Above: Henry Howden on the platform at Skipwith. Lavinia remembers the Nestle's chocolate machine behind with affection, one suspects she was its main customer! Certainly when the passenger service ran takings were not high. The station records show that only two to three pounds worth of tickets were sold each week, with the majority being on Mondays and Saturdays.

Left: Life at the station was obviously relaxed, particularly when the passenger service ended, and there was generally only one train in each direction a day. At Skipwith the Howdens had a number of different enterprises. These included effectively operating a small-holding with goats (seen here with a family friend, Lilian Darnton), chickens and ducks. Henry Howden, like the others in charge of stations, operated a coal business. He would bring in 10 ton wagons of coal, which had to be unloaded in a day, and the coal was sold in the district. The railway only charged for the carriage of the coal, and so any profit was his.

Another enterprise concerned the old brake van body, which can be seen in the background of the photo on the left. This was the second DVLR brake van, which was taken out of service in the late 1920s. It was then brought to Skipwith, wheeled to the site beside the house, and the body jacked up to allow the wheels and axleboxes to be removed.

In the mid 1930s the Howdens operated a fish and chip shop from the van, using primus stoves. The fish, ironically, was delivered by bus. Locals would either come to collect their suppers, or the Howden children operated a delivery service. This enterprise seems to have ended with the outbreak of war.

Above: Of course the odd train did pass through the station, and here is an unidentified class J21 with a passenger excursion, possibly a 'Blackberry Special'.

Above: However, when the trains had gone the yard could become a playground. Here Eric Howden (left) and family friend, Jack Child, are busy playing appropriately with a toy train in the 1930s. A line of coal wagons stand in the siding behind, including two belonging to Fountain & Burnley.

Above left: Italian prisoners of war have been mentioned, and one, Enrico Passery, became a regular visitor to the Howden household. One of the prisoners also presented Mrs Howden with an aluminium cigarette case. Other members of the Howden family also received gifts from the prisoners.
(Above Right Photo: J.D. Stockwell)

Above: The Howden family had other enterprises. Raymond Howden had his own haulage business, and became the official DVLR carrier. On the left is Thomas Howden, Ken Nelson's great-grandfather and a well-known Methodist preacher.

Left: The platelayers' trolley at Skipwith was requisitioned by the Howdens at various times. They used it to go for picnics, or to collect visitors from the bus stop on the Selby Road. Ken Nelson also used it as his personal transport, pumping it up and down the siding in the station yard. Here some family friends, the Shackletons, are preparing for the ride back to Skipwith.

Above: In later years the van body was lowered to the ground, and end doors fitted to turn it into a garage for the Howden's car. Ken Nelson recalls there was also a workbench at the right hand end, which he could stand on to see through the bird cage look-outs. The body was demolished in the 1960s.

Revival

Above: Andrew Barclay No.8, works no.2369, built in 1955, which had worked at the National Coal Board's Barony Colliery, is seen approaching Murton Park with a mixed train on 24 June 2007.   (Photo: J.D. Stockwell)

The story of the revival of the Derwent Valley Light Railway really begins with the foundation of the Yorkshire Museum of Farming at Murton Park, Murton, York. It was established by the Yorkshire Farm Machinery Preservation Society and opened in 1982. They had also acquired part of the DVR's land, along with the remaining track, adjacent to the museum when the line closed.

In September 1983 the DVR presented the museum with the diesel shunter *Churchill*. The locomotive being handed over by Jim Acklam to museum director Brian Horner. They intended to mount a display about the former DVLR and also operate the locomotive on the track.

However, it was not until January 1987 that a Transfer Order was issued. This, as the name implies, transferred the powers of the original Light Railway Orders to the Farming Museum along the length of line it owned. However, little further happened for three years.

The DVLR Revived

In 1989 the Great Yorkshire Railway Preservation Society, who had established a small railway centre at Starbeck on the site of the former locomotive depot, were looking for a new home. This was because the shed site was going to be redeveloped. After some negotiations it was agreed that they should move to Murton Park.

They were joined by a number of individuals from the York area who had either volunteered at the National Railway Museum, or had worked for BR. Then another group from the Hull area who had been involved with the now-defunct Humberside Locomotive Preservation Group became involved.

With the influx of these groups, further locomotives, rolling stock and other materials arrived at the site in the early 1990s. Work also took place relaying the track, as well as building a small workshop and rest room in a grounded coach body. They also constructed a temporary platform. This meant that the first passenger trains could run on August Bank Holiday 1992.

In 1993 regular passenger services began on Sundays and Bank Holidays. These ran along the half mile of track from the western side of Murton Lane to the eastern side of the old Osbaldwick and Murton Road crossing.

At this time the group was still called the Great Yorkshire Railway Preservation Society. However, in 1993 it was

Left: A view of the yet-to-be revived section of the DVLR at Murton Park in March 1982, as seen from the former Murton Lane crossing. The buildings of the new farming museum can be seen on the left. In the distance the by-pass bridge can be seen.
(Photo: David J. Mitchell)

Right: Three years later *Churchill* stands at Murton Park on 6 March 1985. (Photo: R.R. Darsley)

Below: The view from Murton Lane crossing in April 2013. This shows the new mess room building on the left, and the former Wheldrake station building behind. (Photo: I. Drummond)

reconstruction did result in an Ian Allan Heritage Award.

More recent projects have included the construction of a run-round loop at the western end of the line, brought into use in 2010. Meanwhile at Murton Park a further mess building has been built on the east side of the station, in keeping with the DVLR style of buildings. However, the 'jewel' in the crown for the Society to date, has to be the re-construction of the former station building from Wheldrake.

given permission to be called the Derwent Valley Light Railway Society. After a lapse of some twenty years the DVLR was reborn. In the mid-1990s steam also returned in the form of ex-National Coal Board Andrew Barclay locomotive No.8.

Santa Specials have been running on the line since 1993, even through very inclement weather. In recent years several thousand passengers have travelled on them annually, whilst they also provide the opportunity for volunteers to dress up in festive costumes.

Projects

As well as the projects already mentioned, there have been a number of other achievements. The first of these was the re-construction of the former Muston signal box, formerly on the Hull to Scarborough line. Its base is constructed with bricks from Starbeck engine shed's servicing and ash pits. It could be said that as the DVLR only had one signal, a signal box is slightly out of keeping with the original line. But the excellent job of the

Wheldrake Station Building

After the end of the passenger service in 1926, the station building at Wheldrake was sold to a Mr George Simpson. He was the local blacksmith and ran a garage in the village. Through the generosity of the Simpson family the building was donated to the Society in 1995.

The building was dismantled, and in April 1997 work began on rebuilding it at Murton Park. After much hard effort the beautifully restored station building and new platform was formerly opened by the Lord Mayor of York, Rt. Hon. Councillor Peter Vaughan, on Sunday 28 November 1999. It gives a truly authentic feeling to the site.

Locomotives

In addition to *Churchill* the society has developed a large collection of locomotives, mainly industrial diesels. Currently there are two steam locomotives. The first is

Contrasting views at Murton Park

Left: Members start preparing for additional track-laying in 1990. (Photo: P. Green)

Below: The view from the same spot on 10 December 2004. (Photo: Vince Middlebrough)

the aforementioned Andrew Barclay No.8, works no.2369, an 0-4-0 saddle tank built in 1955. The loco came from the National Coal Board East Ayr area, and worked at Barony Colliery among other locations. It was bought by the Hull group in 1982, and was later moved to Murton Park.

The most recent arrival at Murton Park is the steam locomotive *Merlin*, which has come to the line on loan. It was built in 1939 by Peckett & Sons (works no.1967) for the Bristol United Gas Company, and is a 0-4-0 saddle tank.

Among the diesels are two ex-BR locomotives. The first is class 03 former No. 03079. It was built in January 1960 at Doncaster works as D2079, and was eventually sent to Darlington. After being renumbered to 03079 in 1974, it was moved to Gateshead in 1976. After service at Gateshead it then went through Eastleigh works, before being shipped to Ryde on the Isle of Wight in April 1984, where it received a cut-down cab. Having served on the Island for a number of years it was sold for preservation in 1998, and moved to Murton on 6 June the same year.

The second ex-BR locomotive is class 14 D9523, a Type 1 0-6-0 Diesel Hydraulic built at Swindon in 1964. It had a short life in British Rail service being sold to the British Steel Corporation (BSC) in December 1968 and was used

at both BSC Glendon and BSC Corby. In 1981 it was sold for preservation, spending time at various sites until arriving at Murton in April 2011.

Other operational diesels include one with an appropriate local connection to the DVLR. This is a four-wheeled shunter, DS165, built by Ruston & Hornsby in 1953, and delivered new to the British Sugar Corporation in Selby. When the Selby refinery closed in 1981 it was transferred to their York site, where it remained until 1993 when it was donated to the DVLR.

Another recent loan addition is an F. C. Hibberd four-wheel shunter, works no.3777. This was originally built for the Royal Navy Dockyard at Rosyth in 1956 and named *Pluto*. With its distinctive two-stroke Foden engine (105bhp) it has a sound of its own!

One other loco which deserves mention is a Ruston & Hornsby four-wheel shunter of the 88 class, works no. 466630. This was the last loco of this type to be built at Ruston's Boulthan works in 1962. It spent all its operating life at Booths Metals of

Left: Ruston & Hornsby four-wheeled shunter, *Jim*, works no.417892 built in 1959, is seen by the level crossing at Starbeck en-route to Murton Park on 18 August 1990. (Photo: P. Green)

Left: Ex-BR class 14 D9523, built in 1964, at Murton Park on 22 April 2011. (Photo: Vince Middlebrough)

Below: Work in progress on the reconstruction of the former Muston signal box early in 1993. (Photo: P. Green)

Below Left: The completed box on 14 August 2011. (Photo: J.D .Stockwell)

Right: *Pluto*, an F. C. Hibberd four-wheel shunter, works no.3777, built in 1956 for the Royal Navy Dockyard at Rosyth, stands in the run-round loop at the western end of the line on 1 April 2013. (Photo: J.D. Stockwell)

Left: On 10 June 2010 volunteers repainting a tank wagon similar to those which originally ran on the line.

Below: The completed restoration on 2 May 2011.
(Both Photos: J.D. Stockwell)

Rotherham and moved to Starbeck in 1988. Currently it is awaiting an overhaul.

Coaching Stock

There are only three passenger carriages currently on the line, one, an ex-BR Mark One coach, is on loan from the North Yorkshire Moors Railway. The second is a modern 'reproduction' observation car, built in 2003 and named *Sylvia*. Meanwhile the third is probably the most authentic for the old DVLR. This has been constructed from two old NER coaches that were grounded bodies. The reconstructed body runs on a four-wheel chassis from an ex-Southern Region passenger parcel van, the body of the latter being used as a workshop. Painted in a dark blue livery, it is reasonable representation of the former DVLR coaches. There is another ex-NER coach body which is in use as the main mess room. In addition, the Society has a collection of goods wagons which are used on occasional goods train demonstrations.

Centenary Celebrations

Over the weekend of 20 and 21 July 2013 the Society organised a special gala to celebrate the centenary of the original opening. As part of this they brought back to the line two locomotives that used to run on the DVR. These were the steam locomotive *Joem*, and also the former DVR No.2 class 04 diesel shunter now based at The Battlefield Line.

In addition, a recreation of a Ford railbus, based on the DVLR designs, was also present for the event. This made a fine line up of motive power over the weekend.

Right: No.8 makes an impressive display as it emerges from under the by-pass with a *Santa Special* on 19 December 2005.
(Photo: Vince Middlebrough)

To start the event off two grandsons of Lord Wenlock cut a double ribbon, just as had been done a hundred years before. Over the weekend there were many visitors to the line, several with memories of the original DVLR.

The Future

For the future the Society is looking at further developments in the station area, with the provision of a bay platform, a cattle dock and easier access for passengers. There are also plans for an engine shed, for which planning permission has been obtained and fund-raising has begun.

However, the long term goal is to extend the line towards Osbaldwick. This, though, is going to take time and money with a number of significant obstacles to be overcome.

Left: The carriage constructed from the halves of two separate NER coach bodies, mounted on an ex-Southern Railway four-wheel chassis.   (Photo: P. Green)

Right: The yard at Murton Park on 28 November 1999, with another ex-NER grounded coach body acting as a mess room.   (Photo: J.D. Stockwell)

Left: Ex-British Sugar Corporation (BSugarC) shunter DS165 with a passenger train at Murton Park on 5 June 2011. It was built by Ruston & Hornsby in 1953, and in its later years it was based at BSugarC's York refinery until being donated to the DVLR in 1993.

          (Photo: J.D. Stockwell)

Right: Save for the brake van and the locomotive's TOPS number, this could have been a scene from the old DVLR, as 03079 is photographed from the by-pass in April 2007 with a short freight train.

          (Photo: Trevor Humbey)

Left: The frame of the former Wheldrake station building rises at its new home at Murton Park on 12 May 1997.   (Photo: R.R. Darsley)

Right: By August 1998 the building was almost re-assembled.   (Photo: P. Green)

Left: The re-constructed interior to the booking office.   (Photo: P. Green)

Right: The completed building on 12 April 2009.   (Photo: J.D. Stockwell)

Scenes From The Centenary Celebration

Over the weekend of 20 and 21 July 2013 the Derwent Valley Light Railway Society held a special gala to celebrate the centenary of the opening of the line. These are some scenes from the event.

Left: The special headboard worn by *Joem* during the weekend.
(Photo: Stuart A. Stockwell)

Above: The re-enactment of the original ribbon cutting performed by Rev Sir Timothy Forbes-Adam on the left, and his brother Nigel on the right, the latter a former director of the DVLR. They are both the grandsons of the third Lord Wenlock, and so provided a direct link to the formation of the DVLR.
(Photo: Stuart A. Stockwell)

Above: *Joem* with the special centenary train at the western end of the line on Saturday 20 July 2013.
(Photo: J.D. Stockwell)

Above: A reproduction railbus, inspired by the original DVLR railbuses, gave rides during the week-end. It was built by Colin Shutt who constructed a new body on an original Ford Model T chassis, which had been adapted for rail use.

(Photo: Philip Lockwood)

Left: The returnees, ex-DVLR No.2, and *Joem* are seen together on the DVLR for the first time since 1978.
(Photo: J.D. Stockwell)

Bibliography

Books

Branch Line to the Derwent Valley including the Foss Islands branch, V. Mitchell and K. Smith, Middleton Press, 2003

Britain's Rail Super Centres: York, Ken Appleby, Ian Allan, 1993

History of the County of York East Riding Volume Three, Allinson, Baggs, Kent and Purdy, Victoria County History, 1976

North Eastern Railway Brake Vans: A Railway Bylines Special, Ian G. Sadler, Irwell Press, 2003

The Derwent Valley Railway, S.J. Reading, 2nd Edition Ed. D.S.M. Barrie, Oakwood Press, 1976

The Londonderry and Lough Swilly Railway, E.M. Patterson, David and Charles, 1964

Principal Magazine and Journal Articles

A Successful Minor Railway - Profitable Reorganisation on the DVLR, Modern Transport, December 1967

Artistic Railway Station Buildings, The Locomotive, Carriage and Wagon Review, 15 March 1915

Day Trip on the Derwent Valley Light, A. Williams, *Railway World*, December 1960

Derwent Valley Light Railway, C.F. Klapper, *The Locomotive, Carriage and Wagon Review*, 15 February 1929

End of the Line for a Famed Yorkshire Railway, Bill Lang, *Yorkshire Ridings Magazine*, November 1984

Four-wheel Drive Lorry for Road or Rail, The Locomotive, Carriage and Wagon Review, 15 November 1923

Industrial Railways of York, R.R. Darsley, *Industrial Railway Record Special Issue No.139*, January 1995

The Curious Case of the Derwent Valley 'Petrol Coaches', Stephen Garrett, *The Colonel No.98*

The Derwent Valley Light Railway, North Eastern Railway Magazine, September 1913

The Derwent Valley Light Railway, T. Preston, *The Railway Magazine*, October 1913

The Derwent Valley Light Railway, W. Hadfield Craven, *The Railway Magazine*, August 1927

The Derwent Valley Light Railway, J. Dennison and B. Torr, *Model Railway News*, May 1961

The Derwent Valley Light Railway, Robert Sadler, *Railway Bylines*, 1995

The Derwent Valley Light Railway - 60 Years On, R.R. Darsley, *Industrial Railway Record No.51*, November 1973

The Ford Railbuses of the DVLR and Where They Went, E.M. Patterson, *Railway World*, January 1962

Thriving Light Railway, M.P. Jacobs, *The Railway Magazine*, August 1964

Primary Sources

Derwent Valley Railway Company Archive

Archive Records at The National Archive, Kew; East Yorkshire Record Office, Beverley; Hull History Centre; North Yorkshire Record Office, Northallerton; York Explore
Other Records at the National Railway Museum, York

Newspaper articles in *The Yorkshire Gazette, The York Herald, The Yorkshire Evening Press* and *The Yorkshire Post*

Web Resouces

The London and North Eastern Railway Encyclopaedia at www.lner.info
Wikipedia at www.wikipedia.org
Subterranea Britannica at www.subbrit.org.uk

Acknowledgements

The authors would like to acknowledge the assistance of the following people without whom this volume would not have been possible:

All the photographers and copyright holders who have made their work available.

To the staff at Derwent London; Yorkshire Museum of Farming, York; The National Railway Museum, York; The National Archive, Kew; North Yorkshire Records Office, Northallerton; East Yorkshire Records Office, Beverley; The Hull History Centre; The York Press; West Sussex Library Service; York Explore; and York Minster Library.

Former employees, directors, and family members of the DVLR and others, particularly Tom Ashton, David Blackburn, John Bullock, Mrs S.M. Cook, Mrs Patricia Cook, Nigel Forbes-Adam, Trevor Handley, Ken Nelson, Lavinia Nelson, Arthur Richmond, Sheila Robson, Irvine Watson, David and Claire Williamson, plus numerous others, sadly too many to mention, who have given information.

To Laurie Bowles, Alan Doe, Di Drummond, Hugh Norwood and Barbara Plumtree-Varley for proof-reading.

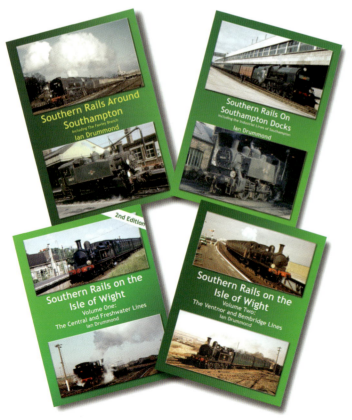
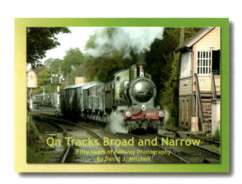